S. S King

Seed Time And Harvest

S. S King
Seed Time And Harvest
ISBN/EAN: 9783744724364

Printed in Europe, USA, Canada, Australia, Japan

Cover: Foto ©Andreas Hilbeck / pixelio.de

More available books at **www.hansebooks.com**

Fraternally Yours,

SEED TIME
AND
HARVEST.

Pictures from the Official Records, wherein are seen
LABOR,
AGRICULTURE,
and TRADE,
Sowing the Seed, in order that
RAILROADS,
BANKS, and
FACTORIES
May Reap the Harvest.

BY S. S. KING,
Author of BOND-HOLDERS AND BREAD-WINNERS.

PUBLISHED BY THE AUTHOR,
KANSAS CITY, KANSAS.

THIS BOOK IS
DEDICATED TO MY WIFE,
WHOSE CONVICTIONS OF RIGHT HAVE EVER BEEN
AN AID AND INSPIRATION TO CORRECT POLITICAL PRINCIPLES;
WHO, SEEKING TO LIGHTEN THE BURDENS OF TOIL,
AND SOFTEN THE SORROWS OF WANT,
SUGGESTED MANY OF THE THOUGHTS HEREIN WRITTEN.

Entered according to act of Congress,
BY S. S. KING,
In the office of the Librarian of Congress, at Washington, D. C.,
in the year 1894.

INTRODUCTORY.

A SCENE FROM AN OLD PLAY.

Place, *A Street in Rome.* Time, *About 490 B. C.*
Enter a company of mutinous citizens, with staves, clubs and other weapons.

First citizen. We are accounted poor citizens, the patricians good. What authority surfeits on would relieve us: if they would yield us but the superfluity, while it were wholesome, we might guess they relieved us humanely; but they think we are too dear: the leanness that afflicts us, the object of our misery, is an inventory to particularize their abundance; our sufferance is a gain to them. Let us revenge this with our pikes, ere we become rakes: for the gods know I speak this in hunger for bread, not in thirst for revenge.

Enter Menenius Agrippa, friend of Coriolanus.

Menenius. Why, masters, my good friends, mine honest neighbors, will you undo yourselves?

Citizen. We cannot, sir, we are undone already.

Menenius. I tell you, friends, most charitable care
Have the patricians of you. For your wants,
Your suffering in this dearth, you may as well
Strike at the heaven with your staves as lift them
Against the Roman state, whose course will on
The way it takes, cracking ten thousand curbs
Of more strong link asunder than can ever
Appear in your impediment. For the dearth,
The gods, not the patricians, make it, and
Your knees to them, not arms, must help. Alack,
You are transported by calamity
Thither where more attends you, and you slander
The helms o' the state, who care for you like fathers,
When you curse them as enemies.

Citizen. Care for us! True, indeed! They ne'er cared for us yet: suffer us to famish, and their store-houses crammed with grain; make edicts for usury, to support usurers; repeal daily any wholesome act established against the rich, and provide more piercing statutes daily, to chain up and restrain the poor. If the wars eat us not up, they will; and there's all the love they bear us.

Menenius. Either you must
Confess yourselves wondrous malicious,
Or be accused of folly. I shall tell you
A pretty tale: it may be you have heard it;
But, since it serves my purpose, I will venture
To stale't a little more.
There was a time when all the body's members
Rebelled against the belly, thus accused it:
That only like a gulf it did remain
I' the midst of the body, idle and unactive,
Still cupboarding the viand, never bearing
Like labor with the rest, where the other instruments
Did see and hear, devise, instruct, walk, feel,
And, mutually participate, did minister
Unto the appetite and affection common
Of the whole body. The belly answered—
"True it is, my incorporate friends," quoth he,
"That I receive the general food at first,
Which you do live upon; and fit it is,
Because I am the store-house and the shop
Of the whole body: but if you do remember,
I send it through the rivers of your blood,
Even to the court, the heart, the seat o' the brain;
And, through the cranks and offices of man,
The strongest nerves and small inferior veins
From me receive that natural competency
Whereby they live: though all at once cannot
See what I do deliver out to each,
Yet I can make my audit up, that all
From me do back receive the flour of all,
And leave me but the bran." What say you to 't?

Citizen. It was an answer. How apply you this?

Menenius. The senators of Rome are this good belly,
And you the mutinous members; for examine

Their counsels and their cares, digest things rightly
Touching the weal o' the common; you shall find
No public benefit which you receive
But it proceeds or comes from them to you
And no way from yourselves.   *   *
But make you ready your stiff bats and clubs;
Rome and her rats are at the point of battle;
The one side must have bale.
      Enter Coriolanus.
 Coriolanus. What's the matter, you dissentious rogues,
That, rubbing the poor itch of your opinion,
Make yourselves scabs?
 Citizen. We have ever your good word.
 Coriolanus. He that will give good words to thee will flatter
Beneath abhorring. What would you have, you curs,
That like nor peace nor war?   *   *   What's the matter,
That in these several places of the city
You cry against the noble senate, who,
Under the gods, keep you in awe, which else
Would feed on one another? What's their seeking?
 Menenius. For corn at their own rates; whereof, they say,
The city is well stored.
 Coriolanus.   Hang 'em! They say!
They'll sit by the fire, and presume to know
What's done i' the Capitol: who's like to rise,
Who thrives and who declines; side factions and give out
Conjectural marriages; making parties strong
And feebling such as stand not in their liking
Beneath their cobbled shoes. They say there's grain enough!
Would the nobility lay aside their ruth,
And let me use my sword, I 'ld make a quarry
With thousands of these quarter'd slaves, as high
As I could pick my lance.

Nearly 2400 years have passed. But Coriolanus, Menenius and the citizens clamoring for food still live.

CORIOLANUS AND THE ROMAN CRY FOR BREAD.

CHAPTER I.

THE CONCENTRATION OF WEALTH, CONSIDERED WITH REFERENCE TO LOCALITY.

In the spring of 1892 the writer hereof published a little pamphlet entitled "Bondholders and Breadwinners." The author thereof was very careful that every fact stated and figure given should be absolutely and incontrovertibly correct. Dealing with United States statistics of wealth, the Government Census of 1890 was taken as the authority for all the figures given. The entire success of that undertaking has abundantly rewarded the effort made to be fair, candid and truthful. Indeed, the author believes it pays to be as fair, candid and truthful in the discussion of politics as in the discussion of any other matter. Not a figure therein given has been challenged, and no statement of fact has been shaken. The most that any enemy of that work has succeeded in doing is to dispute the correctness of some of the author's conclusions based on the facts and figures therein.

The wonderful success of the publication referred to has been sufficient to warrant this undertaking. The large sales reached, the high commendations received and the consciousness of great good accomplished all combine to justify the author in the belief that he had then discovered matters of sufficient moment to interest the people, and to be worth the telling. So he thinks of the present matter in hand. As that was candid and truthful, so shall this be. As that has stood as a strong plea for the people, and stood unshaken, so shall this.

In order that my readers may the better understand this work, I desire that they should know something of that. It was a startling story. As our friend Menenius said,

> It may be you have heard it;
> But since it serves my purpose, I will venture
> To stale't a little more.

The purpose of "Bondholders and Breadwinners" was to show the concentration of wealth—not in the hands of individuals and corporations so much as in the favored sections of the country. I there sought to show and did show that through the unjust operations of unholy laws certain portions of the Nation, unduly favored by wicked legislation, accumulated vast wealth during the decade from 1880 to 1890, while other sections less favored by legislation, but which in fact *produced* the greater wealth, were deprived of their fair proportion of wealth-gain. For example it was shown that:

INDIANA, ILLINOIS, IOWA, NEBRASKA, LOUISIANA,

THE HARVEST OF SECTIONS. 11

MISSISSIPPI, ALABAMA, GEORGIA and NORTH CAROLINA, nine great producing states, having 58 times as much land and 7 times as many people to cultivate it, gained less wealth in the decade from 1880 to 1890 than the one little railroad-owning state of MASSACHUSETTS. This proportion of people ▮ and land ▮ in the East was enabled to accumulate more wealth than this proportion of people ▬▬ and land ▬▬▬▬▬▬ ▬▬▬▬▬▬▬▬▬▬▬ in the West and South.

INDIANA, ILLINOIS, IOWA, NEBRASKA, LOUISIANA, MISSISSIPPI, ALABAMA, GEORGIA, NORTH CAROLINA, KANSAS, KENTUCKY and FLORIDA, twelve great producing states, with 14 times as much land and 4 times as many people to cultivate it, gained less wealth in the period named than the one manufacturing state of PENNSYLVANIA. This proportion of people ▮▮ and land ▬▬ in the East was able to accumulate more wealth than this proportion of people ▬▬▬ and land ▬▬▬▬▬▬▬▬▬▬▬▬▬▬▬▬▬ ▬▬▬▬▬▬▬▬ in the West and South.

INDIANA, ILLINOIS, IOWA, NEBRASKA, LOUISIANA, MISSISSIPPI, ALABAMA, GEORGIA, NORTH CAROLINA, KANSAS, KENTUCKY, FLORIDA, TENNESSEE, VIRGINIA and WEST VIRGINIA, fifteen great producing states, with 16 times as much land and 4 times as many people to cultivate it, gained less wealth in the period named than the Banking and Bondholding state of NEW YORK.

This proportion of people ▬ and land ▬ in the East was able to accumulate more wealth than this proportion of people ▬▬▬ and land ▬▬▬

▬▬▬ in the West and South.

INDIANA, ILLINOIS, IOWA, NEBRASKA, LOUISIANA, MISSISSIPPI, ALABAMA, GEORGIA, NORTH CAROLINA, KANSAS, KENTUCKY, FLORIDA, TENNESSEE, VIRGINIA, WEST VIRGINIA, MISSOURI, ARKANSAS, SOUTH CAROLINA, DELAWARE, MARYLAND and OHIO, twenty-one producing states forming the great body of the Union, a wonderland of diversified resources, with 6 times as much land and twice as many people to cultivate it, were able to accumulate one-half as much wealth in the period named as the nine North Atlantic states of MAINE, NEW HAMPSHIRE, VERMONT, MASSACHUSETTS, CONNECTICUT, RHODE ISLAND, NEW YORK, PENNSYLVANIA and NEW JERSEY. This proportion of people ▬▬ and land ▬▬▬▬ in the East, accumulated twice as much wealth in the period named as this proportion of people ▬▬▬ and land ▬▬▬▬

▬▬▬ in the great producing section of the country.

The great producing body of the Union is comprised in these 21 states. Texas was not included because its wealth-gain was derived from ranch stock rather than agriculture. This is not saying that Texas is not a great agricultural state. But in addition to its agriculture it has had the other great industry of stock raising on wild lands. Vast fortunes have been made from that industry, and these vast fortunes give Texas a great wealth-gain. The gain is not from agriculture, as Texas people will freely admit. The three Northern pine-tree states of Minnesota, Wisconsin and Michigan were not included in these comparisons, because their large wealth-gains were derived from protected lumber monopolies rather than agriculture, as the farmers of those states well know. The new states and territories to the westward were not considered, because too young to furnish valuable lessons. The purpose was to contrast those states engaged in Agriculture with those engaged in Manufactures, Transportation and Banking.

It was largely of the same states of which I wrote, that Senator Ingalls wrote a few months later. I quote from his splendid article in Lippincott's Magazine, June, 1892: "Sparsely inhabited, with rude and unscientific methods, its resources hardly touched, the states of the Mississippi valley last year produced more than three-quarters of the sugar, coal, corn, iron, oats, wheat, cotton, tobacco, lead, hay, lumber, wool, pork, beef, horses and mules of the entire country, together with a large fraction of its gold and silver. Their internal commerce is already greater than all the foreign commerce of the combined nations of the earth." This being true, and it is true, one would naturally conclude that a portion of the world so fertile as this, a portion that can feed, warm and clothe the world, should receive at least its fair proportion of the world's accumulation of wealth.

But that it does not is shown by the facts stated above and by others which follow. The wealth produced by the diversified industry of these 21 states remains not with the producers, but is drawn away to the North Atlantic states by reason of their Manufacturing, Railroading and Banking interests, through the operation of unjust legislation that favors those interests. In addition to this drain to the East, the wealth produced in this great producing district has been drawn also to the North. The protected pine lumber monopolies have levied a tribute as onerous as that paid to the East. Millionaire fortunes have been accumulated to the northward as well as to the eastward, not worked from the soil, but worked from the workers of the soil.

These constant drains of wealth from the Produce District (the 21 states) into the Wealth District (the 9 states) and into the Lumber District (the 3 states) were illustrated by a cut which I am constrained to reproduce here, even at the risk of being wearisome. These great wrongs on the people connot be too frequently impressed upon their attention.

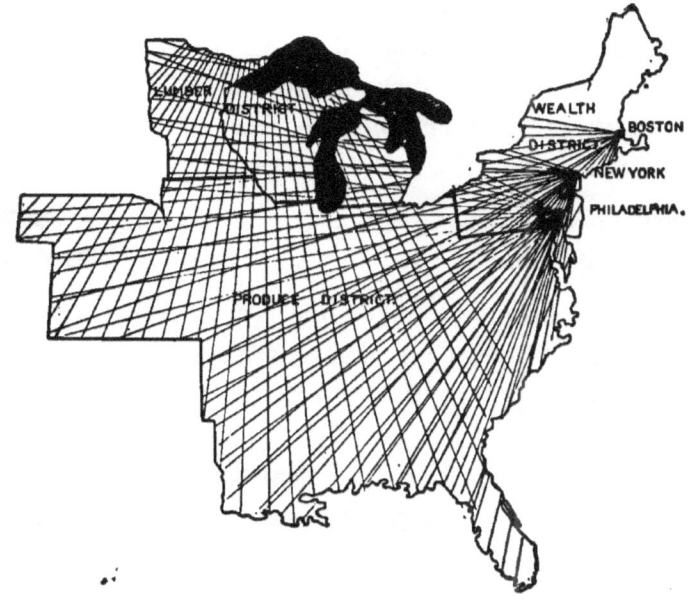

Texas and the states and territories to the westward of Minnesota, Nebraska and Kansas are not shown in this illustration. Some are too young to be of any service in these comparisons; the population of others has increased so largely; so much land has changed from government to individual ownership; some are so remote from the body of the nation, and in others the causes operating are so different from the causes operating in the Mississippi valley that to include them in this illustration or discussion would be manifestly unfair and tend to obscure rather than enlighten.

But of those portions of the country shown in the foregoing chart:

The Lumber District (the three pine-tree states of Minnesota, Wisconsin and Michigan) with 7 per cent of the entire population of the nation held 12 per cent of the wealth-gain of the nation from 1880 to 1890, represented thus:

    Population.. ▅
    Wealth-gain.. ▅

The Wealth District (the nine North Atlantic states named) with 29 per cent of the entire population of the nation held 41 per cent of the total wealth-gain, represented thus:

    Population................................... ▅▅▅▅▅▅▅▅▅▅
    Wealth-gain .... ▅▅▅▅▅▅▅▅▅▅▅▅▅▅

The Produce District (the 21 states mentioned forming the body of the nation) with 56 per cent of the entire population kept only 23 per cent of the total wealth-gain, represented thus:

    Pop.... ▅▅▅▅▅▅▅▅▅▅▅▅▅▅▅▅▅▅▅▅
    Wealth-gain... ▅▅▅▅

Thus is seen the exceedingly unequal distribution of the wealth-gain considered with reference to the geographical divisions indicated. This Produce District, the 21 states, can feed and clothe the world. Its 56 per cent of the entire population of the nation, living on fruitful soil, should accumulate at least its proportionate percentage of the wealth-gain, instead of only 23 per cent. The 29 per cent of the entire population, living among the worn-out hills of new England, should not accumulate more than their proportionate percentage of wealth, and when that percentage goes up to 41, something is wrong somewhere. It behooves the patriot to seek to discover where the wrong is. It is not in these figures. They are official. Those relating to population are from Official Census Bulletin No. 16, and those relating to wealth from No. 104.

Since "Bondholders and Breadwinners" was written Mr. Superintendent Porter of the Census Bureau has issued a further bulletin pertaining to the wealth of the nation. Its purpose is to correct certain supposed errors in No. 104. The changes however are not important, and would not materially alter the results I have given. As my former work is still being published from the plates prepared on the basis of the figures given in bulletin No. 104, I refer to the same figures now, rather than to the slightly altered ones.

Mr. Superintendent Porter has added to the wealth of some of the western states, in this corrected bulletin, for the reason which I quote from him as follows: "The figures of 1880 are taken from the report of the Tenth Census, and in the states where values of railroads are known to be included therein for that year, viz., California, Indiana, Iowa, Kansas and South Carolina, like figures have been included in the figures of 1890 so as to secure proper comparison between the two periods." We know that the railroads of the Mississippi valley are owned in the East. The increase, therefore during the decade, increases the wealth-gain of the East rather than of the West, and it is believed that were this additional wealth, added to the wealth of the states that really own it, the showing would be still more favorable to eastern concentration than indicated in the figures taken from bulletin No. 104.

I have been thus particular in epitomizing a portion of my former publication in order that the reader may the better understand the exposition which follows. We have seen the unequal flow of wealth to certain states. It goes to the favored classes who happen to live there. The purpose of the following pages will be to show who those favored classes are, and the manner in which their great wealth is accumulated at the expense of the producers.

CHAPTER II.

THE CONCENTRATION OF WEALTH, CONSIDERED WITH REFERENCE TO CLASSES.

Much has been said and written on this subject of concentration of wealth in the hands of a few people, and for years we have heard and read of "The rich growing richer and the poor growing poorer." The statement can also be made and fully sustained that the number of very rich is yearly growing larger, and the number of very poor is increasing with like rapidity.

The highest and best official authority is sought in giving all the figures herein. Mr. Geo. K. Holmes, of the Census Bureau, has recently greatly assisted these researches by a splendid article published in the *Political Science Quarterly* for December. His figures are of course authoritative and authentic, and as near official concerning the matters of which he treats as we may hope to get. The writer hereof acknowledges his indebtedness to Mr. Holmes for much useful information. From that valuable article we learn the following facts:

Total families in United States............ 12,690,152
Number of families living on farms............ 4,500,000
Number of families living in homes other than farms........ 8,190,152
Of the families on farms, 32 per cent are tenants.
Of the families living in other homes, 63 per cent are tenants.
Of the farm-owning families, 30 per cent have their farms mortgaged.
Of the home-owning families, 29 per cent have their homes mortgaged.
Average amount of farm mortgages, $1130.
Average amount of home mortgages, $1139.

Let us look at this statement in all its startling import. This is the land of freedom! The land of homes! And yet, the land of the homeless! If the reader will figure on the percentages given by Mr. Holmes as I have quoted them, he will be rewarded for his pains and startled with this result:

Farm families who own no homes............ 1,440,000
Other families who own no homes............ 5,159,796

Total families who own no homes............ 6,599,796
Farm families who own mortgaged farms *............ 752,760
Other families who own mortgaged homes *............ 720,618

Total homeless and mortgaged families............ 8,073,174

---

*The reader will find some difficulty in figuring these percentages, both here and in Mr. Holmes' article, to produce the results given above. If he deduct 32 per cent from 4,500,000, and then take 30 per cent of the remainder, he will have considerably more than 752,760 farm families owning mortgaged farms. And if he deduct 63 per cent from 8,190,152, and then take 29 per cent of the remainder, he will have more than 720,618 families owning mortgaged homes other than farms. Mr. Holmes, in dealing with mortgaged farms and other homes, owned by the occupants, deals only with those worth less than $5,000. Of these farms and homes he finds 82 per

Here we find a clear majority of all the families of the United States without homes, and nearly two-thirds without clear homes! The inspiration to patriotism is love of home. The love of country is a blighted and blasted affection unless it first buds and blossoms about the home. A homely yet forcible assurance has been given us by some one to the effect that men are not disposed to battle very much in defense of the boarding house. Neither will they fight very valiantly for the home of some one else. The home, not the house, must develope the patriotic spirit. If the rich shall fear the growth of anarchy in the Republic, let them by wholesome legislation, put into the hands of the poor the fair and reasonable possibility of acquiring and owning the home that shall be their little world. Loving that little home and through it the Nation, the protection and defense of both shall be their highest glory.

Mr. Holmes, in this connection, shows that 6,599,796 families of the United States, being 52 per cent of the total families, own less than one-twentieth of the total wealth. Is not this most startling? Look at it! Consider it in all its hideousness! More than one-half of the people own only 5 per cent of the wealth!

---

cent of each worth less than $5,000. Hence the reader must take 30 per cent of 82 per cent of the remainder in one case, and 29 per cent of 82 per cent of the remainder in the other, in order to get the correct number of mortgaged farm and home families. If the reader shall think this is not very clear he is referred to Mr. Holmes' article where, it is feared, he will not find it much clearer.

The other half, less than half, own 95 per cent of the wealth! If we state this surprising truth in the shape of an illustration, it will furnish a valuable object lesson, thus:

▬▬▬▬▬▬▬▬▬▬▬▬▬▬ this part of the families owns this part of the wealth ▬

▬▬▬▬▬▬▬▬▬▬▬▬▬▬ this part of the families own this part of the wealth ▬▬▬▬

▬▬▬▬▬▬▬▬▬▬▬▬▬▬▬▬▬▬▬▬
▬▬▬▬▬▬

Thus we see how small a portion of the wealth is owned by half the families—little more than half. We will now increase the percentage of families, and see how small a part of the wealth is owned by nearly all the people. Mr. Holmes says, "91 per cent of the 12,690,152 families own no more than 29 per cent of the wealth, and 9 per cent of the families own about 71 per cent." Another object lesson, thus:

▬▬▬▬▬▬▬▬▬▬▬▬▬▬▬▬▬▬▬▬

▬▬▬▬▬▬▬▬ this part of the families owns this part of the wealth ▬▬▬▬▬▬▬▬

▬▬▬▬ this part of the families owns this part of the wealth ▬▬▬▬▬▬▬▬▬▬▬▬
▬▬▬▬

Thus we have the families of the Nation divided into two classes, designated as the rich and the poor. But Mr. Holmes proceeds further, and from among the rich evolves another class, viz., millionaires. Of these he finds 4,047 families whose average wealth is $3,000,-000, making a total of $12,000,000,000, or one-fifth of the entire wealth of the country. Think of this! 4,047 families own 12 billion dollars' worth of property, while 6,599,796 families own less than 3 billion dollars' worth.

But to quote from Mr. Holmes again: "We are now prepared to characterize the concentrated wealth of the United States by stating that 20 per cent of it is owned by three-hundredths of one per cent of the families; 51 per cent by 9 per cent of the families (not including the millionaires); 71 per cent by 9 per cent of the families (including the millionaires); and 29 per cent by 91 per cent of the families."

The three-hundredths of one per cent mentioned above is the 4,047 millionaire families. That part of the entire number of families is so small as to destroy the usefulness of diagrams. Three-hundredths of one per cent! One thirty-third of one per cent! Or, one in 3300! It is so small as to be scarcely discernible.

We have now developed four classes from the article quoted; the very rich, 4,047 millionaire families constituting one thirty-third part of one per cent of the families and possessing 20 per cent of the wealth; the rich, 1,092,218 families, being about 9 per cent of the total and possessing 51 per cent of the wealth; the home-owners of moderate means, 4,994,091 families, being 39 per cent of the total and possessing 24 per cent of the wealth; the homeless, 6,599,796 families, being 52 per cent of the total and possessing 5 per cent of the wealth. Our diagrams representing this classification (combining the first two classes into one, because the millionaire class is too small a percentage to be represented in a diagram) will appear thus:

▅▅▅▅▅ this part of the families, 9 per cent (the rich and very rich) owns this part of the wealth, 71 per cent
▅▅▅▅▅▅▅▅▅▅▅▅▅▅▅▅▅▅▅▅▅▅▅▅▅▅▅▅▅▅
▅▅

▅▅▅▅▅▅▅▅▅▅▅▅▅▅▅▅ this part of the families, 39 per cent (home owners) owns this part of the wealth, 24 per cent ▅▅▅▅▅▅▅

▅▅▅▅▅▅▅▅▅▅▅▅▅▅▅ this part of the families, 52 per cent (homeless) owns this part of the wealth, 5 per cent ▅▅▅

Let this be stated still another way so as to impress the frightful picture of these great inequalities of wealth distribution as strongly as possible on the reader's mind, if the foregoing illustrations have in any manner failed:

No. Families.	Class.	Average per Family.	Total for class.
4,047	Millionaire	$3,000,000	$12,000,000,000
1,092,218	Rich	28,735	30,500,000,000
4,994,091	Home-owners	2,915	14,560,939,343
6,599,796	Homeless	418	2,795,898,000

Is there not food for the thoughtful mind in these figures? Think of it! The average wealth of all the families in the United States (about five persons to the family), according to Mr. Holmes, and according to all Census figures, is about $4,728. Thus, then, the 4,047 millionaire families own the shares of 2,538,071 families. But, again, it is the millionaire himself, not the family, who owns and controls the vast wealth. Of the 4,047 families there are 4,047 persons who own as much wealth as all the people in 2,538,071 families or 12,690,355 people. That is to say, of this millionaire class, each average millionaire possesses as much wealth as the average 3,135 people in the other class! And here my diagrams must fail again. I cannot contrast 1 with 3,135 very well. If I made one side of the contrast large enough to be seen, the other would be too large for this work. So I will have to let the reader make his own comparison.

If, then, the financial legislation of the past 30 years has been such that in the wealth distribution of this Republic, one person has been enabled to accumulate as much wealth as 3,135 persons, and to extend the operation of these conditions to 4,047 cases, does the reader fear a change in legislation? Can the economic conditions be made worse than they are? How?

Another interesting question in this connection is as to the sources from which these vast fortunes were derived. Census reports, perhaps, cannot show this. But Mr. Holmes quotes the New York *Tribune's* statement, with apparent approval, showing the particular channels through which the great wealth flowed to these 4,047 peculiarly favored families. The following table is reproduced from that article:

Land and its exploitation	825
Natural and artificial monopolies	410
Agriculture, ranch stock, sugar, etc., often with land	86
Trade and manufactures, often with land and securities	2,065
Interest, profit and speculation not otherwise mentioned, often with land	536
Inheritances, otherwise unexplained	34
Miscellaneous, often with land	70
Unknown	21
Total	4,047

While this table is useful in showing the fountains from which the vast fortunes have flowed, or, rather, the channels through which they have flowed, it would be still more valuable had it gone further into details, if such were possible.

LAND AND ITS EXPLOITATION, 825! It is difficult to understand just what the compiler meant by the word "exploitation." It is believed to be used in the sense of acquiring land and then deriving the largest financial benefit from it by such work as developing mines, felling forests, etc. The gentlemen who "exploited" lands, and accumulated vast fortunes from their operation, generally obtained them at merely nominal prices. While millions are landless, houseless and fireless the "exploiters" are permitted to form monopolies in land, lumber and fuel, building the princely fortunes of the favored classes while the hollow eye and bloodless hand of want are seen at every turn.

NATURAL AND ARTIFICIAL MONOPOLIES, 410! These natural and artificial monopolies may be designated as: railways, canals, ferries, telegraphs, telephones, electric-lights, gas-works, water-works, patents, copyrights, etc. There are, perhaps, others that do not occur to the writer at this time, but not of great importance or general use. The one great monopoly that stands out pre-eminently is that of the railways. Nearly all of these 410 great fortunes were made through this one of the monopolies.

AGRICULTURE, RANCH STOCK, SUGAR, ETC., OFTEN WITH LAND, 86! It was a happy thought of the compiler, after starting this class with Agriculture, to put in some ETCETERA. And it was a happy use of language that selected the word Agriculture rather than Farming. In more recent nomenclature I believe it is proper to speak of the farmer as one who farms the land, while an agriculturist is one who farms the farmer. But as it is exceedingly difficult to imagine a case where a farmer has become a millionaire through the regular channels of cultivating the land to grain, cotton, tobacco, fruit, garden truck, or any other farm product; or, in devoting the farm to live stock or dairy products, it is easy to understand that the agriculture meant is of the ranch-stock-sugar-etcetera variety.

TRADE AND MANUFACTURES, OFTEN WITH LAND AND SECURITIES, 2,065! By far the largest class of all. And these millionaire fortunes have all been accumulated during the latter third of the Republic's life. It may be doubted whether a single one in this class was produced during the first two-thirds. And why not then as well as now? I quote again from Mr. Holmes: "A new country, like the United States, in its past decades, affords many opportunities for making fortunes that are rarely or never found in the older countries. The opening of mines, the cutting of forests, the building and consolidating of railways, the rise in land values in growing cities, *the expansion of manufacturing and trading demands in a rapidly-increasing population*, all these stimulate the initiator to play for great stakes. But the period of such chances and opportunities is transitory; pioneers cannot be followed by pioneers. As time passes fortune-building on the whole settles down to an investment of the saving of a moderate rate of interest."

This being true, then the first two-thirds of our National life should naturally have been more condusive to fortune-building than the latter third, unless the latter period has been improved for this purpose by artificial means. I suspect the application of such artifices in these later years. In the former years natural laws favorable to fortune-building failed to make millionaires Now, in spite of less favorable natural conditions, they come trooping by thousands. If the production of millionaires and paupers be a misfortune there must be error somewhere in the political economy we have practiced.

INTEREST, PROFIT AND SPECULATION NOT OTHERWISE

MENTIONED, OFTEN WITH LAND, 536! This is the banking and bondholding business of the country. "The best banking system on earth," shout the alleged patriots of all parties, and the writer has heard this so often that he is inclined to believe it is the best—for the banker. A banking system that makes millionaires at this rate should strongly commend itself to the kind and enthusiastic approval of—usurers. Not to borrowers.

But enough now of Mr. Holmes and his excellent exposition of certain forcible and fruitful truths. These copious extracts have been made and commented on in order to set before the reader in the strongest possible light certain existing conditions—to show the deep and still deepening gulf between Lazarus and Dives, and to ask: Shall we plunge blindly in like the ill-fated cuirassiers into the sunken roadway of Ohain, or shall we bridge it? Shall another Menenius again declare that "Rome and her rats are at the point of battle?"

CHAPTER III.

THE CONCENTRATION OF WEALTH THROUGH RAILROAD TRAFFIC.

Railway Statistics form a very interesting feature of the Eleventh Census. The Bureau has published ten bulletins in relation thereto, prepared by Henry C. Adams, special agent in charge of the Division of Transportation.

Mr. Adams believes that the conditions in this country are so incongruous that the railroad business of the entire Nation, considered as an entirety, would be useless, and so proceeds to classify the roads by groups. Ten of these groups are thus classified in the ten bulletins, and are arranged as follows:

Group I. The New England States.

Group II. New York, New Jersey, Pennsylvania, Delaware, Maryland and part of West Virginia.

Group III. Ohio, Indiana, Southern Peninsula of Michigan, and parts of Pennsylvania and New York.

Group IV. Virginia, West Virginia, North Carolina and South Carolina.

Group V. Kentucky, Tennessee, Mississippi, Alabama, Georgia and Florida.

Group VI. Illinois, Northern Peninsula of Michigan, Minnesota, Wisconsin, Iowa, North Dakota, South Dakota and Missouri.

Group VII. Nebraska, Montana, Wyoming and parts of North Dakota, South Dakota and Colorado.

Group VIII. Missouri (South of Missouri River), Arkansas, Kansas, Indian Territory, Colarado South of Denver and New Mexico North of Santa Fe.

Group IX. Louisiana, Texas and part of New Mexico.

Group X. California, Oregon, Washington, Idaho, Nevada, Arizona, Utah and part of New Mexico.

These statistics furnish much useful information, and form a valuable addition to the railroad literature of the country. The several matters treated are official and as nearly correct as we can hope ever to obtain.

The Economy of Labor forms one important feature in these bulletins; and though the reference I am about to make to that feature may be a digression from the purpose of this work, yet I am impelled to make it in the interest of Labor. Generally, I believe, Census figures show an increase of wages in 1890 over 1880. And for this the various Labor Organizations of the country deserve congratulation. I am not writing of economic conditions since 1890, but during the last census decade. But any advance of wages from 1880 to 1890 was not made by the voluntary action of Capital; nor by reason of an increasing demand for Labor; nor by reason of a decrease in the supply of Labor. If the conditions of Labor were improved it was all due to its efforts in making its just demands on Capital and Legislation.

But while wages increased, the relative opportunity of earning wages decreased. While the worker was enabled to earn more, the army of unemployed was augmented by great accessions of new recruits. So much more labor accomplished by one man, and so much greater proportion of laborers unable to find employment, are the results of more approved methods and more improved machinery. This cause and this effect are written on every page of our National history. If the earning capacity of the man has increased, it were a gross injustice if his wages should not also increase.

The earning capacity of employees of railroads in 1880 and 1890 is shown in the bulletins by the number of men employed and the amount of work accomplished. In 1880 one man employed in conducting transportation was necessary to move a certain number of tons of freight or a certain number of passengers one mile. In 1890 he was able to accomplish much more. The nine Groups (these particulars being missing in Group VII) show the following as the comparison of the work accomplished by each employee in these two years named, in tons of freight carried one mile.

Group I in 1880,	88,234,	in 1890,	90,961.	Increase	3	per cent
" II "	219,679,	"	233,321.	"	6	"
" III "	251,932,	"	300,288.	"	20	"
" IV "	126,985,	"	234,450.	"	86	"
" V "	125,845,	"	201,737.	"	61	"
" VI "	204,493,	"	237,698.	"	16	"
" VIII "	153,391,	"	197,473.	"	28	"
" IX "	126,513,	"	180,905.	"	43	"
" X "	130,340,	"	200,838.	"	54	"
Total 9 men "	1,427,412,	"	1,877,771.	"	32	"

The same comparisons with reference to the passenger traffic show the number of passengers carried one mile by the work of each employee in 1880 and 1890.

Group I in 1880,	54,863,	in 1890,	60,583,	Increase	11	per cent
" II "	29,050,	"	33,093,	"	14	"
" III "	33,154,	"	36,747,	"	11	"
" IV "	22,770,	"	30,726,	"	36	"
" V "	22,603,	"	31,641,	"	41	"
" VI "	30,526,	"	35,227,	"	17	"
" VIII "	32,587,	"	35,451,	"	9	"
" IX "	23,963,	"	29,419,	"	23	"
" X "	59,530,	"	78,986,	"	14	"
Total 9 men "	309,046,	"	361,873,	"	17	"

Thus is seen that the earning capacity of all these employees engaged in the work of conducting transportation, considered with reference to the whole country, has increased 32 per cent as to freight traffic and 17 per cent as to passenger traffic, doubtless more than is the increase in the rate of wages.

And here, while engaged in this digression, I am compelled to present another very forcible truth, viz., that while our own railroads pay higher wages they really pay less for labor than those of other countries. This seems paradoxical. But it is a fact. The railroads of the United States pay higher wages to their employees than are paid by the railroads of Great Britian, Belgium, Russia, Germany, or France; and yet by reason of the much greater number of men employed on the roads of all those European countries, their expenditure per mile for labor is much in excess of our roads. In a valuable work recently written by ex-Governor Larrabee of Iowa,* and which I shall take some liberties with in the further progress of this treatise, this fruitful truth is set forth. It is not necessary to compare the figures as to all the nations mentioned, as those of Great Britian alone will answer. It costs the railroads of Great Britian $6,000 per mile to pay their employees, an average wage of $335 per annum for each of their 18 men per mile; while the roads of the United States pay $2625 per mile, an average of $555 per annum for each

---

* "The railroad Question, A Historical and Practical Treatise on Railroads, and Remedies for their Abuses, by William Larrabee, late Governor of Iowa. Chicago: The Schulte Publishing Company." The writer of this desires to commend Governor Larrabee's great work to all thinking people, believing it to be the most entertaining, profound, just and patriotic discussion ever presented on this great question. Its truths are so elegantly and so ably presented that the work furnishes a world of delight and a store-house of information to the reader. It costs $1.50. If you want to understand railroad methods, read it, by all means.

of their 5 employees per mile.* On this important fact Governor Larrabee says:

"The train men of Europe work less hours and earn less per capita for their employers than do the train men of this country. The average annual gross earnings per employee on sixteen of the leading lines of Great Britian, as shown by Mr. Jeans, appear to be $975, against $1,600 on fifteen leading lines of the United States, while the average net earnings per employee are $465 on the British lines against $720 on the American lines; making a difference in favor of this country of 70 per cent in gross earnings and 53 per cent in net earnings. If American labor is more expensive, it is also more efficient than labor is elsewhere."

Hence it would appear that by reason of greater efficiency of American labor, the railroads are actually operated at less expense than British roads, or other European roads; and that this efficiency of our labor is still increasing. It ought, then, to reasonably appear that the railroads of this country are in a prosperous condition, as compared with the roads of the other countries named, so far as expenditures for labor are concerned.

Bulletin No. 192 of the Eleventh Census gives the total wealth-gain of the United States, from 1880 to

---

* If the hyper-critical reader shall object to this because 6,000 is not the product of 335 x 18, and 2,625 is not the product of 555 x 5, let him solace himself with the thought that Governor Larrabee found 18 and 5 to be the nearest whole number that could express the number of employes per mile, and kindly omitted the fractional part.

1890, based on actual values rather than assessed values, as $20,006,000,000. This is so near an even 20 billions that we may call it that—an even 2 billions per year. This wealth-gain shows a percentage of gain of a fraction over 45 per cent for the 10 years, or a gain of 4½ per cent per annum. This fact is an important one to be borne in mind. It may here raise a question in the inquiring mind as to the measure of success that shall probably attend the effort of the great multitude of borrowers who believe they can do a legitimate business on capital that costs them 10, 12 or 15 per cent. To the writer it seems to be as immutable as the law of Heaven that where one may succeed by chance ninety and nine must fail through the operation of natural laws.

Mr. Adams in bulletin No. 46, pertaining to Group I of railways, makes this surprising statement: "It is a little surprising to notice that corporate investments for roads outside of New England are over three times as much per mile of line as investments of New England railways." Perhaps this apparently surprising fact may be accounted for in the further fact that New England roads were built and put in operation at a time when Capital was not fully acquainted with the efficacy of "water." Perhaps New England owners of New England roads are satisfied to let their New England neighbors simply pay interest and dividends on actual bonds and stocks, requiring the blood of only the West and South in atonement for the extravagant use of "water" in other roads. At any rate there is no gainsaying the proposition that these Western roads that our New England friends own cost less to build and equip than their New England roads. If they are capitalized at three times as much it is all due to the blessed and all-conquering power of "water."

In bulletin No. 46 Mr. Adams says: "From a public point of view no question is of more importance than the valuation of railway property. There are several rules for arriving at such valuation, one of which is to capitalize at an assumed rate of interest the earnings of railway capital. Adopting this rule for the New England railways, it would be difficult to find more satisfactory data for the calculation than that submitted in the income account, since the earnings and expenses per mile of line which it exhibits are a true average based on ten years of actual operations. The amount of earnings on railway capital is of course equal to the amount of interest, rentals and dividends paid as these items appear on the books of operating roads. For the ten years ending 1889 these payments amount to $169,263,553.67, which, reduced to the basis of twelve months' operations and assigned to a mile of line, show that New England railways paid yearly to the owners of railway capital the sum of $2,676.10 per mile. This sum, capitalized at the rate of 5 per cent, gives $53,522 as the value of railway property per mile of line."

Observe this reasoning. After paying all expenses of maintenance and operation—repairs, renewals, improvements, wages, insurance, and taxes—in short, every possible expenditure that can be deducted from the gross earnings, a certain sum is left as net earnings. And this sum is sufficient to pay 5 per cent on $53,522. Hence this may be taken to be the value of New England railways. Not their cost or their capitalization; but their value, because they are profitable at that valuation. This 5 per cent is net, remember. That is a liberal rate of interest, above all expenses. We speak of 10 per cent on investments. But that is gross earnings of capital. Out of that taxes must be paid, insurance kept up and all sorts of hazards taken. And the 5 per cent is more than the National gain.

On the basis quoted above, allowing 5 per cent net as a very fair return for capital, Mr. Adams finds the railroads of the several Groups to be worth the figures given below, and he finds them to be worth those prices, not because they cost that much, nor because they are capitalized at those figures, but because they are profitable at the prices named. The valuations according to his calculations are as follows:

Group I, $53,522; Group II, $96,052; Group III, $35,026; Group IV, $19,559; Group V, $26,617; Group VI, $38,316; Group VII, $29,114; Group VIII, $35,309; Group IX, $22,423; Group X, $45,896.

This will make, if the reader cares to average it, something over $40,000 per mile of road. That is to say that the entire railroad mileage of the United States (good, bad and indifferent) existing in 1890 (about

160,000 miles) were worth $40,000 per mile because, for a continuous period of ten years, they had been profitable at that price.* The entire value of the railroads of the United States (not their cost or capitalization) in 1890 can thus be set down at $6,400,000,000.

The capitalization of the roads in 1890 may be set down in round numbers at $60,000 per mile. Thus the 160,000 miles given by the Census Bureau at the beginning of 1890 were capitalized at a total of $9,600,000,000.†

The cost of these 160,000 miles of railway at the several times they were built is a more difficult question, perhaps, than any other connected with the railroad question. The general consensus of opinion among those best posted places the figures between $20,000 and $30,000. Governor Larrabee, in the work already mentioned, declares $25,000 to be a liberal estimate of the average cost. This makes the total cost $4,000,000,000.

The present cost of railroad building is still more interesting. Governor Larrabee deals extensively with this question. He quotes from Henry Clews in his "Twenty-Eight Years in Wall Street," who declares that "For $15,000,000 a road could be built where it had cost the Union Pacific $75,000,000." The Governor

---

* If the reader cares for exact figures they are 159,215 miles at an average value of $40,183, making $6,397,736,345.

† The mileage given in the various Railway Magazines for 1890 is 163,420 and the total capitalization is placed at $9,746,141,603.

refers to the fact that "Very recently the Union Pacific Railroad Company proved, before the Board of Equalization at Salt Lake City, by the testimony of engineers, that the average cost per mile of the Utah Central line was only $7,298.20." Quoting from C. Wood Davis, the Governor shows us these facts: "Some years since the Santa Fe filed in the counties on its line a statement showing that at the then price of labor and materials (rails were double the present price) their roads could be duplicated for $9,685 per mile, and, the materials being much worn, the actual cash value of the road did not exceed $7,725 per mile." "In 1885 the superintendent of the St. Louis and Iron Mountain Railway, before the Arkansas State Board of Assessors, swore that he could duplicate such a railway for $11,000 per mile." But where is the use of multiplying examples or cumulating evidence? It is believed that no one will seriously dispute the proposition that with the present low prices of rails and other materials, together with the greatly increased economy of labor, the railroads of the United States could now be built at an average cost of not more than $15,000 per mile, making a total of $2,400,000,000.

Thus, then, we may conclude as to the 160,000 miles of railroad dealt with in the Census of 1890:

Cost to build on basis of present prices,	$2,400,000,000.
Cost when they were built,	$4,000,000,000.
Present Value on 5 per cent net basis,	$6,400,000,000.
Present Capitalization,	$9,600,000.000.

Let the reader understand that the above figures are not the mere guess-work of the writer. They are not the wild vagaries or the unsupported theories of a novice in railroad matters. The present cost, it will be seen, is based on the sworn testimony of railroad men. The original cost is the estimate of the father of tariff legislation in Iowa, a gentleman who has given almost a life-time study to railroad matters, and been one of the highly respected Governors of that great state. The value based on net earnings is the result of the labor of Mr. Adams of the Census Bureau. The capitalization is that given by the railroad companies themselves, and published in the railroad magazines of the country.

No one, it is believed, will deny to the railroad companies the right to receive fair and reasonable returns on the vast capital necessary for the construction and operation of their roads. Such returns ought to be commensurate with the general wealth-gain of the whole country. Why it should be any higher than such average gain the writer cannot see. Such average gain is, as before stated, 4½ per cent. But say the railroad owners shall receive 5 per cent net, after paying all possible expenses, including taxes. On what basis shall they receive such returns? Shall it be on the cost of the roads to construct them now? The price of other property is generally based on present cost. That is to say, present cost of production generally determines prices. A building is worth about what it would cost to construct another like it, with an allowance, perhaps, of some interest on the capital during the period of its construction. Why should not the same rule apply to railroad property? On this basis the railroad companies should receive $120,000,000 net earnings per year on their present probable cost of $2,400,000,000.

But we will be more than fair with the railroads. Let us say the companies should receive 5 per cent net on the cost of the roads at the times they were built. This is saying that the business of the country shall save the companies harmless from the great depreciation of values and pay all the profit they would have been entitled to had no such depreciation occurred. This is certainly a more liberal and gracious concession than the Railroads, Bankers and Manufacturers would be willing to make to the Laborers, Farmers and Tradesmen were the rights of the latter being considered. By this rule the masses of the people should pay to the railroad owners $200,000,000 per annum as fair returns on their investments. But they did pay (not for just one exceptional year, but an average for 10 years) 5 per cent net on $40,000 per mile. Hence, in 1890 they paid this return on a total value of $6,400,000,000, a total payment in net earnings of $320,000,000. Will not the reader candidly admit that this is too much? Figuring on this basis of the original cost of the roads, we find that the people paid in one year $120,000,000 above legitimate profits—above 5 per cent net on the original high-priced cost of construction.

But this is not all. There are certain large payments that are deducted from the gross earnings and included in the operating expenses that should more properly be called net profit. For example, a President or General Manager not infrequently receives a salary of $50,000 per year. The bulk of such princely compensation goes to such favored officer, not because his talents are worth such compensation—not because his abilities are superior to the abilities of other men—but because he is so related to the ownership of the road that he and his friends can vote as large a salary as they like. The corporation Counsellor whose annual round up is $100,000 receives it because he is sufficiently close to certain stockholders to get it. And the many million dollars' worth of free transportation furnished in little pasteboard passes to the friends of the stockholders are part of the price which the masses of the people pay for their freight and passenger traffic. And so it may be said that the following large sums should be added to the net profit of the railroad business, they being now deducted as expenses from the gross earnings. The estimate of the several items was made by C. Wood Davis and quoted with approval by Governor Larrabee. The following are some of the more important:

Estimated attorneys' fees and legal expenses	$12,000,000
Estimated amount of free pass evil	30,000,000
Estimated payment to high-priced managers, etc.	4,000,000
Estimated payment to Presidents and other officers	25,000,000

There must be presidents, general managers, attorneys and general officers to conduct the business of the roads. But is it not safe to say that a large portion of these several sums is given through favoritism? A portion of the passes is given in payment for legitimate work done or expenses paid. But it is entirely safe to say that more than half the free transportation is given through favoritism or in payment for corrupt work. Of these items we can with entire safety add $40,000,000 to the other $120,000,000 of excess above legitimate profits, making a total excess of $160,000,000 per annum.

Thus we can say that the railroads of the United States in 1890 drew from the people in net earnings $360,000,000. This sum is $240,000,000 in excess of their legitimate profits if we base their present worth on the present cost, and is $160,000,000 in excess of such legitimate profits if their worth be based on original cost. The reader can take his choice of the method of computing the extortion.

We thus see that $4,000,000,000 of the wealth of the Nation (the one-fifteenth part) has taken to itself in net earnings $360,000,000 of the wealth-gain of 1890.

But why protest? What rights have the masses of the people that they may hope to enforce against the corporations? Thousands of railroad owners are aided in their work by thousands of political leaders whose tones are tuned by the rythmetic flow of gold. They defy the people. They demand to know of you Laborers, Farmers and Tradesmen what you are going to do

about it? Why presume to lift your voice against a
power stronger even than the Government—a power

>>Whose course will on
The way it takes, cracking ten thousand curbs
Of more strong link asunder than can ever
Appear in your impediment.

CHAPTER IV.

CONCENTRATION OF WEALTH THROUGH BANKING.

The writer approaches this chapter on Banks and Banking with fear and trembling. The Banker is such an exalted personage in the community by reason of his highly respectable calling; honored by those who have money, and feared by those who must borrow of him; if he is a National Banker he belongs to a system so revered by the "patriots" of both the great parties, so sacred in the minds of many people that "No image of some marble saint niched in cathedral aisles is hallowed more from the rude hand of sacrilegious wrong." The thought that the writer's hand, if it should write aught against this sacred institution, may be classed as rude and the work it does as sacrilegious, is peculiarly oppressive.

Who has not heard, over and over again, the declaration made by citizens of great information, apparent honesty and supposed patriotism, that the National Banking system is the best banking system ever devised by the wisdom of man? This has been told so often by these persons—these moulders of public opinion—that many have come to believe it. And no wonder. The writer is disposed to believe the system to be the best on earth—for those engaged in it.

The report of President Harrison's Comptroller of the Currency, Mr. Edward S. Lacey, for 1890, helps to confirm this oft-repeated declaration. Mr. Lacey says:

"Shareholders have, as a rule, received satisfactory returns on their investments, and the people at large have been faithfully served. The growth of the system furnishes indubitable proof that it is admirably adapted to the requirements of a commercial people, and that its merits are becoming more generally recognized and appreciated. * * * The increasing popularity of the system will be apparent when it is observed that during the present report-year 307 new associations have joined the system, and that these are distributed among 41 states and territories. * * * It thus appears that the persistent attacks made upon the national system, based, as a rule, upon misinformation and mainly incited by baseless predjudices, have failed to bring about its destruction or prevent its steady, indeed, rapid extension in all parts of the United States. The involuntary confidence reposed by the people at large in the associations of which it is composed, growing stronger each succeeding year, has at last compelled their establishment in many countries long falsely taught to regard them as instruments of oppression and inimical to the public good. So the material and financial interests of the citizen prove, in time, more potent than the political predjudcies of the partizan."

There is a sort of exultation in the tone of this utterance that almost suggests to the average reader that possibly similar rejoicing might follow the operation of one whose peculiar financial system had been carried to a successful issue in holding up an express train and appropriating the surplus. There is a sort of a breezy bulldozing about this language that suggests danger ahead if Mr. Lacey should be given the power to direct affairs. There is an ill-concealed condemnation of all those whose "baseless prejudices" have failed in their "persistent efforts," and lofty contempt for those whose "misinformation" has been the menance of these sacred institutions.

But notwithstanding all this, it is refreshing to learn from Mr. Lacey of the "confidence reposed by the people at large," and to be assured that this sublime confidence is "growing stronger each succeeding year." True, the confider might enjoy his bestowal of confidence to a greater extent if it were a voluntary surrender on his part, instead of involuntary—if he had freely entered into an admiration of the system instead of being forced into it. Most men like to act freely in the bestowal of love, admiration or confidence. They do not like to be drafted against their will into these conditions. When two men were quarreling a newly-elected Justice commanded the peace, and to prevent its breach, shot both the disputants. They died with "involuntary confidence" in the efficacy of the judicial act. Perhaps the Comptroller's approved method of forcing "involuntary confidence" is somewhat similar.

This sweet "involuntary confidence" which had been "growing each succeeding year" would have had a happier ending had it died prior to 1893. It is believed the Comptroller could not write so beautifully of "confidence" in 1893 as he did in 1890. But happily for Mr. Lacey his official duties have glided away into the dead past, and another hand writes the report for 1893. President Cleveland's youthful Comptroller, James H. Eckles, made the last report December 4, 1893. For some reason Mr. Eckles omits any and all reference to Mr. Lacey's "confidence." Even "involuntary confidence" is wholly ignored. Mr. Eckles, however, gives us some figures that may very well take the place of the confidence lecture. Indeed it is safe to say that these facts have taken the place of confidence. And it is eminently proper that they should. The last report shows the suspensions of National Banks during the year ending October 31, 1893, together with their capital stock. Following are the figures, the states being arranged by the writer in groups as classified by Census groupings:

STATES.	NO. BANKS SUSPENDED.	CAPITAL STOCK.
Maine (none)		
New Hampshire	2	$250,000
Vermont (none)		
Massachusetts (none)		

States.	No. Banks Suspended.	Capital Stock.
Rhode Island (none)		
Connecticut (none)		
New York	2	500,000
New Jersey (none)		
Pennsylvania	1	50,000
North Atlantic Division	5	$800,000

States.	No. Banks Suspended.	Capital Stock.
Delaware (none)		
Maryland (none)		
District of Columbia (none)		
Virginia (none)		
West Virginia (none)		
North Carolina	2	$300,000
South Carolina (none)		
Georgia	4	675,000
Florida	2	200,000
South Atlantic Division	8	$1,175,000

States.	No. Banks Suspended.	Capital Stock.
Ohio	2	$ 180,000
Indiana	7	1,000,000
Illinois	4	2,150,000
Michigan	3	215,000
Wisconsin	5	625,000
Minnesota	5	2,400,000
Iowa	6	575,000
Missouri	3	1,300,000
North Dakota	3	400,000
South Dakota	3	225,000
Nebraska	6	800,000
Kansas	8	880,000
North Central Division	55	$10,750,000

STATES.	NO. BANKS SUSPENDED	CAPITAL STOCK.
Kentucky	6	$2,300,000
Tennessee	6	2,750,000
Alabama	4	550,000
Mississippi	1	60,000
Louisiana (none)		
Texas	12	1,480,000
Oklahoma	1	50,000
Arkansas	1	500,000
SOUTH CENTRAL DIVISION	31	$7,690,000

STATES.	NO. BANKS SUSPENDED.	CAPITAL STOCK.
Montana	10	$1,875,000
Wyoming	2	250,000
Colorado	16	3,600,000
New Mexico	2	225,000
Arizona (none)		
Utah	3	250,000
Nevada (none)		
Idaho (none)		
Washington	14	1,735,000
Oregon	6	800,000
California	6	1,200,000
WESTERN DIVISION	59	$9,935,000
GRAND TOTAL	158	$30,350,000

This is rather a startling picture. During the period of one year 158 banks belonging to this "Best banking system on earth" suspended payment, and wrought incalculable financial ruin to multitudes of confiding people. Their aggregate capital was $30,350,000. How much their liabilities were—how much of the money of depositors was tied up in these suspensions, Comptroller Eckles fails to show. Why he fails to show this important matter is not clear, in view of the many other details shown in his report. However, as the deposits of the National Banking system at the time of the suspensions were more than double their capital stock, it is safe to presume the same was the case with the suspended banks, thus indicating more than $60,000,000 of deposits placed for a time beyond the reach of depositors. It is believed this sum was enough to point toward a diminution of "involuntary confidence," and perhaps raise some "involuntary doubt" concerning this " Best banking system on earth."

The reader will thus see that "all is not gold that glitters" even about a National Bank. Some of it may be the gilded tinsel of "involuntary confidence." Their foundation is not one that can stand the financial storm when it comes. In spite of supposed careful Governmental supervision, even honest bank managers will sometimes fail, and the system is seen to offer little security for the confiding depositor.

One remarkable fact appears in connection with the record of suspended banks as given above—a fact in entire harmony, however, with other facts herein stated. Seeing the Concentration of Wealth in the extreme East as shown in Chapter I, and in the hands of the Eastern millionaire classes as shown in Chapter II, the reader may think there is no need of bank failures in those states or among those people. There was no need, and there were no failures, comparatively. Think of it. The

9 little states forming the North Atlantic Division (Maine, New Hampshire, Vermont, Massachusetts, Rhode Island, Connecticut, New York, New Jersey and Pennsylvania) *holding more than one-half of the capital stock of the entire National Banking system*, suffered only 5 National Bank suspensions, involving only $800,000 capital.

All the rest of the country, possessing a little *less than half of the capital stock of the system*, suffered 153 suspensions, involving $29,550,000 capital.

And yet we hear and read heart-rending accounts of the financial distress in the East that has involved the Manufacturing and Railroad interests in utter and almost irremediable ruin. Why do not the banks show it? They fall when their support falls. The thrifty banker of Venice knew how it was when he sorrowfully told the court:

> You take my house when you do take the prop
> That doth sustain my house.

No, no! The financial distress was not in the East among the Railroad owners and Manufacturers, where the Bankers stood firm. It was in the West and South among the Laborers who were compelled by stress of circumstances to draw out their little savings to live upon; among the Farmers whose products would yield no compensating returns, and among the Tradesmen whose success or failure depended on the ability of the others to buy and pay. And the financial distress of all these three classes in the West and South forced the failure of banks in the West and South, 153 in a total of 158. The panic tells the story of each succeeding year, and tells it with an emphasis. Those who create the wealth are forbidden through unjust laws, to participate in its enjoyment or share in its possession.

It is not the purpose of this work to enter into a discussion of the financial crimes of legislation that have been committed against the people for the benefit of the great Banking power of the country. A chapter might be written on each of a score of wicked enactments passed by Congress since the creation of National Banks. The act itself that created them, in giving them the power to expand or contract the currency of the country at will, and thus absolutely control the destiny of the whole people so far as finances can control, was a reckless disregard of the rights of the masses, amounting at least to crimnal carelessness on the part of the law-makers; the exception clause in the greenback whereby one kind of money was made for the rich and another kind for the poor, was a wrong to every man who was compelled to accept payment in depreciated currency; the act for the pretended purpose of Strengthening the Public Credit was a withering fraud on the producers of the Nation, and was passed for the purpose of strengthening Public Plunder rather than Credit; the Demonetization of Silver in 1873; the contraction and destruction of the currency from 1866 to

1875; the forced resumption of specie payments in 1879; the final enforced cessation of silver coinage; the various unnecessary sales of interest-bearing bonds, including the Carlisle crime of 1894—these and many other infamous acts of legislation have been lobbied through Congress in the interest of the arrogant and oppressive money power of the country.

Does the reader believe the National Banking system has been entitled to all the favorable legislation it has received? Let us see whether or not it could have found a reasonable prosperity short of the general destruction wrought to other industries. May it not be that National Banks have been made too prosperous to accord with other enterprises? The issue for February 28, 1894, of "The American Banker, a Weekly Financial Journal Devoted to the Interests of Banks, Bankers and Investors," published in New York, contains some quotations of the value of stock in National Banks. In view of the present financial ruin that threatens many of the interests of the country, these quotations will be useful as showing how well the Banks fare. Following are some of those quotations given, the Banks named below all belonging to the National system:

Broadway.	Par value of shares	$	25.	Now bid per share			$200
Butchers & Drovers	"		25.	"		"	170
Chatham	"		25.	"		"	340
Chemical	"		100.	"		"	4,000
City	"		100.	"		"	425
First	"		100.	"		"	2,500

Mechanics	Par value of shares	$	25.	Now bid per share	$180
Chase	"	"	100.	" "	450
Gallatin	"	"	50.	" "	280
Garfield	"	"	50.	" "	350
Hanover	"	"	100.	" "	300
Importers & Traders	"	"	100.	" "	550
Lincoln	"	"	100.	" "	500
New York County	"	"	100.	" "	575
Park	"	"	100.	" "	250
Second	"	"	100.	" "	300
Sixth		"	100.	" "	300

The list given above is not all the Banks quoted. It comprises those that are quoted the highest. But in all the long list of New York Banks there is not one quoted below par—all the way from par up to the magnificent figures of $40 in value for $1 of investment, as in the case of the Chemical.

But National Bank prosperity is not confined to New York. Fancy values are quoted in the paper named all over the country. Like the ivy the National Bank can be found flourishing where no other life is seen. Here are a few specimen quotations:

At Chattanooga $100 shares sell for $240; Cincinnati, $320; Denver, $250; Des Moines, $320; Indianapolis, $320; Knoxville, Tenn., $300; New Orleans, $344; Omaha, $225; Philadelphia, $380; Pittsburgh, $700; Washington, $400. This list might be extended indefinitely, but doubtless this is quite sufficient.

How would Laborers, Farmers and Tradesmen like to operate under legislation sufficiently favorable that their investments in the shop, the farm and store, besides paying excessively liberal dividends from year to year, should increase in value many fold, as the stocks of National Banks have done? It is believed that Labor would be less wearisome, and farming more beautiful if their results could be measured by the same increase as National Bank investments. If toil shall pay as great annual dividend each year as Banks have paid, and the toiler see his home increase in value from year to year as Bank stocks have done, instead of decrease until it reaches down to the mortgage debt, then things would be more fairly adjusted than they are. And why not? Why should the toiler sow and the Banker reap where he has not sown?

The total capital stock of all the National Banks from September 1, 1889 to September 1, 1890, is reported by Comptroller Lacey at $615,405,515 for the first half of that fiscal year and at $634,773,746 for the latter half —thus the average capital for the year was $625,089,630.

The gross earnings on this capital were, for the year named, $144,614,053, equal to more than 23 per cent.

Why are not these gross earnings the correct basis when considering the rate of interest? If a Laborer, by some peculiar stroke of fortune, should save a little money, and loan it out at the current rate of 8 or 10 per cent interest, or deposit it in a savings bank at 4 per cent, such rate is the earnings of his capital. From that he must pay taxes on such capital, provide for any losses that may occur, and compensate himself for any time or labor consumed in attending to his capital so invested. And so it is with the Farmer and Tradesman. We make laws against excessive interest, and almost all the States have fixed a limit beyond which persons shall not contract. Of the 44 States, 35 have such laws against usury. In 32 of the States 10 per cent per annum is the maximum rate. And this rate, remember, is the *gross* return allowed for the capital loaned, not the *net*. The lender, in a suit to recover a debt, is not allowed to say that he has devoted his time to the business of loaning his money and should have something for that; that he has paid taxes on his capital loaned and suffered losses which must be returned to him, above the 10 per cent. The rate fixed by law is the maximum gross rate, and the owner must not be permitted to receive compensation for labor, taxes or losses beyond that rate. Why make a different rule for the Banker? Why shall not his time, his taxes and his losses be "thrown in" as well as the time, taxes and losses of the other person? Why shall the Banker be better than the people? Shall the creature be greater than the creator? Shall the stream rise above its source? It seems so.

But let us be more than fair with the Banks as we were more than fair with the Railroads. There is no reason for unfairness with any of these favored classes. To be more than fair we can still find more than enough of which to complain. These National Banks deduct from their *gross* earnings, "Losses and Premiums," $21,292,732; also, "Expenses and Taxes," $51,265,758, leaving the *net* earnings, $72,055,563, *or 11½ per cent net profit after paying all expenses*. It is thus seen how evenly the Banks divide their earnings into two parts, one-half going to operating expenses and the other half going to net profit—11½ per cent to each. It is probable that some of these enormous expenses *should* be charged off in considering profits. But is it not possible that all should be. Fancy Bank salaries, like fancy Railroad salaries, are paid to the owners of the capital, or to those who stand near enough to the owners to get it. Let us see. In the average National Bank of, say $100,000 capital, the president or vice-president (possibly both) will receive salary, large or small, according to the degree of supervisory care they bestow on the business; then come the cashier, assistant cashier, teller and several accountants, with good salaries, a total of $5,000 to $8,000, that is as much a part of the earnings of Banking capital as any other part is. Take the conservative middle ground and say that in this Bank $6,500 goes to these salaries, we then have 6½ per cent to be added to the 11½, making 18 per cent as the annual returns of National Banking capital.

Is not this reasoning fair? If not, why not? Wherein is it false, faulty or unfair? Custom does not allow the Farmer to pay himself a salary out of the products of his farm, leaving the remainder for profits; perhaps for the very excellent reason that there would be no remainder. He puts his labor in with his capital and tries to make some return on the two combined—and generally fails. Why should a different rule apply to the Banker?

On the basis, then, of their reported net earnings and the estimated salaries of officers, making in all 18 per cent per annum, the National Banks of the country are accumulating, on their capital of $625,089,630, the astounding income of $112,516,137.

Besides these National Banks there were in 1890 a large number of State Banks, Loan and Trust Companies, Savings Banks (stock), and Private Banks. These are reported by the Comptroller as possessing capital stock to the amount of $326,656,607. There is no official statement as to their earnings.

For some reason not known to the writer the deposits in these Banks are much larger in proportion to their capital than are the deposits of the National Banks. The National Banks in the year in question, with $625,-089,630 of capital held $1,564,845,174 of deposits. The other Banks named above with $326,656,607 of capital held $1,203,255,549. Thus the Banks other than National, with only 52 per cent as much capital as the Nationals, yet held 77 per cent as much deposits.

A quotation from Comptroller Lacey's report will not be out of place here. He says:

"The deposits of a National Bank are now its principal source of profit. Originally they realized a profit upon circulation as well as deposits. The high rate of premium commanded in the market by the interest-bearing bonds of the United States, which are required to be deposited by these banks as security for their circulation, has rendered the issue of circulating notes, in most localities, unprofitable. Hence National Banks now organizing issue only so much of circulation as is obligatory under the law. They are fully cognizant of the fact that no profit will be realized on account of the right to issue notes, and proceed in their organization mainly because of the gain to result by reason of deposits."

The reader will have no difficulty to discover another reason, in addition to that given by Mr. Lacey, for the decrease in the National Bank circulation. It reached its highest volume in 1874, being then in round numbers 340 million dollars. It decreased from that year onward until in 1890 the amount was less than 123 millions. The Banks had learned they could gain more from a contracted circulating medium than from an expanded one. And thus they, in order to decrease the money of the country, began to do their share toward contraction. How well they have done it is written on every foreclosure proceeding and in every forced sale throughout the land.

But the source of a National Bank's profits are the deposits, Mr. Lacey tells us. There is probably no reason why the other Banks should not make as large a proportionate gain on their deposits as the Nationals. True, the Nationals make a portion of their profits on

Government Bonds, but relatively that portion is not large now that their circulation has fallen off so largely. Having a less rigid supervision, perhaps, than the Nationals, in some of the States, and with more liberty as to certain classes of investments, it is safe to say that the earnings of other Banks from deposits are proportionately as large as the Nationals. This would give to the Banks other than National annual profits of $86,637,425. This sum added to the profits of the National Banks ($112,516,137) makes a total profit of $199,153,562 as the income derived by the Banks and Bankers from the people of the Nation.

Think of it? Here is less than one billion of the total wealth of the United States (less than one-sixtieth) engaged in Banking, and this accumulates 200 million dollars (one-tenth) of the total wealth-gain. Remember the general wealth-gain is 4½ per cent. Banking, occupying as favorable a position as other businesses, should receive not more than 50 million dollars, instead of 200 millions. But allowing this business double the profits that go to the general business of the country, and it then takes 100 million dollars too much from the industries of the Nation. Our law-makers have been doing what the Roman citizen charged against his law-makers: "Make edicts for usury, to support usurers; repeal daily any wholesome act established against the rich, and provide more piercing statutes daily, to chain up and restrain the poor."

CHAPTER V.

CONCENTRATION OF WEALTH THROUGH MANUFACTURES.

The reader, I know, has been greatly interested thus far in noting the concentration of wealth, considered with reference to geographical divisions as well as with reference to classes, as shown in the preceding chapters. If he has hitherto given no attention to these matters he has been surprised as well as interested by by these revelations. As we have discovered that a large proportion of these millionaire fortunes is derived from manufactures, I will now ask the reader's attention to some important truths concerning that great field of American enterprise.

The Census of 1890 is much more complete than any that has preceded it, in going into the details of many industries. The reports of the Eleventh Census would have been very valuable assistants to the student of economics, had they been published in reasonable time. They will still be valuable aids hereafter if they shall ever be published. Whether or not they ever will be published I am not advised. It has frequently been said, and apparently with some show of reason, that the full publication is being withheld by those who control National partizan politics, because it is not desired by them that voters shall become too familiar with many of the potent facts therein revealed. Be that as it may, it is certain that the work of the Census takers performed nearly four years previous to this writing has not yet been given to the general public in the shape of published volumes. However, some hundreds of different bulletins, pertaining to many different matters, have been issued and distributed to editors, bankers, lawyers, etc. In writing "Bondholders and Breadwinners," early in 1892, it was there said: "The earnest reformer of things politically evil will need no text book but Mr. Porter's Eleventh Census Report, and not having that in time for next year, will be able to proceed very nicely with the bulletins that are being sent out." The language is appropriate now for this volume as it was then for that.

From the large number of bulletins that have been sent out from the Census Bureau pertaining to manufacturing interests, there being one for every principal city and town in the United States, the following figures are taken, concerning the manufacturing interests of the ten largest cities. Ten cities are taken because that number is sufficient for the purpose of illustration. The entire list of all the cities in the Nation is not taken because this volume is not sufficiently elaborate to admit of doing so. The ten largest cities are taken because their manufacturing interests are the largest and most diversified, and consequently furnish the fairest basis for calculation. I believe this will be conceded as fair. Thus, then, the ten cities and their manufacturing business during the Census year of 1890, the cities named in the order of their size, and their business given as follows:

BULLETIN No. 211—CITY OF NEW YORK.

Capital invested in Manufactures, $420,238,602.
Value of manufactured products.................................$763,833,923
Wages paid..$228,537,295
Cost of materials used........................... 357,086,305
Miscellaneous expenses......................... 60,228,425   645,847,025
Profit...$117,986,898
Percentage of Profit on Capital, 28.

BULLETIN No. 222—CITY OF CHICAGO.

Capital invested, $292,477,038
Value of Manufactured Products.................................$632,184,140
Wages paid..$119,146,357
Cost of materials used........................... 386,814,848
Miscellaneous expenses......................... 41,550,761   547,511,966
Profit...$ 84,672,174
Percentage of Profit on Capital, 29.

BULLETIN No. 244—CITY OF PHILADELPHIA.

Capital invested, $362,895,272
Value of Manufactured Products.................................$564,323,762
Wages paid..$132,436,268
Cost of materials used........................... 302,623,539
Miscellaneous expenses......................... 39,505,579   474,565,386
Profit...$ 89,758,376
Percentage of Profit on Capital, 22.

Bulletin No. 234—City of Brooklyn.

Capital invested, $125,849,052
Value of manufactured products $248,750,184
Wages paid .... $ 61,975,702
Cost of materials used 137,325,749
Miscellaneous expenses 14,824,466   214,125,917
Profit .... $ 34,624,267
Percentage of Profit on Capital, 27.

Bulletin No. 170—City of St. Louis.

Capital invested, $133,292,699
Value of manufactured products $225,500,657
Wages paid .... $ 52,170,536
Cost of materials used 120,887,355
Miscellaneous expenses 17,381,274   190,439,165
Profit .... $ 35,061,492
Percentage of Profit on Capital, 26.

Bulletin No. 232—City of Boston.

Capital invested, $116,644,490
Value of manufactured products $208,104,683
Wages paid .... $ 54,636,695
Cost of materials used 104,631,879
Miscellaneous expenses 21,399,162   180,667,736
Profit .... $ 27,436,947
Percentage of Profit on Capital, 24.

Bulletin No. 269—City of Baltimore.

Capital invested, $82,526,344
Value of manufactured products $140,401,026
Wages paid $35,377,538
Cost of materials used 73,614,829
Miscellaneous expenses 8,093,119   117,085,486
Profit .... $ 23,315,540
Percentage of Profit on Capital, 28.

BULLETIN No. 246—CITY OF SAN FRANCISCO.

Capital invested, $65,612,049
Value of manufactured products.................................$131.263,713
Wages paid...............................$29,860,057
Cost of materials used............................ 77,188,061
Miscellaneous expenses........................... 7,901,164   114,949,282
Profit..$ 16,314,431
Percentage of Profit on Capital, 25.

BULLETIN No. 270—CITY OF CINCINNATI.

Capital invested, $89,886,796
Value of manufactured product........................$178,650,185
Wages paid...............................$43,934,384
Cost of materials used............................ 83,090,968
Miscellaneous expenses........................... 18,338,352   145,363,704
Profit..$ 33,286,481
Percentage of Profit on capital, 37.

BULLETIN No. 231—CITY OF CLEVELAND.

Capital invested, $56,826,496
Value of manufactured products.................................$104,199,169
Wages paid...............................$27,596,408
Cost of materials used............................ 58,763,062
Miscellaneous expenses........................... 4,690,406   91,049,876
Profit..$ 13,149,293
Percentage of Profit on Capital, 23.

The total amount of capital invested in the manufacturing enterprises of these ten principal cities reaches the astonishing figure of $1,746,248,838. The value of the manufactured products of these ten cities, above the cost of wages, raw materials and miscellaneous expenses reaches the further astonishing figure of $475,494,709. This latter sum appears as the profits of the year 1890, and makes the average profits of these vast enterprises something over 27 per cent.

Extra Census Bulletin No. 67, issued by Mr. Carrol D. Wright, Commissioner of Labor in charge of the Census Bureau, dated March 15, 1894, was received by the writer when this much of this chapter had been written. Previous to the issuance of this bulletin the information given by the Bureau was that pertaining to particular cities or particular industries. No totals had been found. When, therefore, this work was undertaken, indeed, when this chapter was commenced, it was the intention, after giving the preceding statistics concerning the 10 principal cities, to then found the further statements concerning Manufactures on estimates based on these cities. But fortunately this official bulletin now supplies the missing link and renders estimates unnecessary. This bulletin is a complete compilation of all the manufacturing industries of the entire United States.

From this official document we learn some wonderful facts, the first of which is that Capital employed in Manufactures has increased 121 per cent from 1880 to 1890. This is a wonderful fact, in connection with the further facts that during the same time population has increased 25 per cent and the Nation's wealth 45. The total capital in this great branch of American industry is now reported to be the astounding sum of $6,524,-375,305. Is it strange that there should be stagnated business in those industries where capital had been more than doubled during a decade showing only an increase of 25 per cent in population? Certainly, while the capitalists assure the producers that their cheap prices are due to overproduction, it would be well for them to think of the same cause operating with Manufacturers. And yet we do not find the effects nearly so disastrous with them as with the Farmers.

As this chapter deals with the profits of the Manufacturers, it is well that the reader should understand the calculations by which the Census Bureau arrives at its conclusions. The details of all manufacturing enterprises are as in the example here given. This example is taken from New York, and relates to the business of 1,554 establishments for the manufacture of men's clothing (factory product). The detail statement is given as follows:

CAPITAL EMPLOYED:
 Hired property.....................$18,809,332
PLANT:
 Land............................. 86,000
 Buildings......................... 503,000
 Machinery, tools and implements...... 691,025
LIVE ASSETS:
 Raw materials.................... 5,682,026
 Stock in process and finished........... 12,445,012
 Cash, bills and accounts, and all sundries not elsewhere reported........ 10,374,660

Total Capital............................$48,591,055

Aggregate value of manufactured goods.................$68,630,780
WAGES PAID..............................$22,548,892
MATERIALS USED:
 Principal materials............ 30,853,293
 Fuel................................ 64,310
 Mill supplies..........................
 All other materials................. 322,847

MISCELLANEOUS EXPENSES:
  Amount paid for contract work.........$2,322,308
  Rent.. 1,253,017
  Power and heat.................................   244
  Taxes... 14,289
  Insurance... 107,843
  Ordinary repairs of b'ld'gs and m'c'hy   46,349
  Interest on cash used in business......... 32,780
  All sundries not elsewhere reported..... 350,694 $57,976,866
Net Profit..$10,653,914
Per cent of profit on Capital (other than hired property which received its profit in rent) 37.

The above is taken as a sample of one year's operations in those large enterprises. The critical reader will doubtless consider that every possible charge has been made and deducted from the output of the enterprises, and that the remainder is fairly stated as the net profits.

Upon that basis census figures were made. Having read and studied the foregoing condensed statement concerning the business of the ten principal cities, the reader will doubtless be interested in the business pertaining to the principal industries, considered with reference to the entire country. The figures relating to twenty of the leading industries in the United States, based on the same system as given in the preceding example, are as follows:

> Lumber and other mill products from logs or bolts, capital invested, 496 million dollars, profits 13 per cent.
> Foundry and Machine shop products, 382 milllions, 18 per cent.

HARVEST OF THE MANUFACTURERS. 71

Iron and Steel, 373 millions, 9 per cent.
Cotton Goods, 354 millions, 8 per cent.
Malt Liquors, 232 millions, 18 per cent.
Flouring and Grist mill products, 208 millions, 14 per cent.
Agricultural Implements, 145 millions, 12 per cent.
Woolen Goods, 130 millions, 11 per cent.
Men's Clothing, factory product, 128 millions, 30 per cent.
Lumber, planing mill products, including sash, doors and blinds, 120 millions, 19 per cent.
Carriages and Wagons, including custom work and repairing, 104 millions, 20 per cent.
Slaughtering and Meat Packing, Wholesale, 98 millions, 30 per cent.
Boots and Shoes, factory product, 95 millions, 27 per cent.
Paper, 82 millions, 15 per cent.
Leather, tanned and curried, 81 millions, 20 per cent.
Worsted Goods, 68 millions, 13 per cent.
Furniture, 66 millions, 24 per cent.
Tobacco, Cigars and Cigarettes, 59 millions, 30 per cent.
Silk and Silk Goods, 51 millions, 24 per cent.
Hosiery and Knit Goods, 50 millions, 19 per cent.

It is useless to pursue this matter in detail, as these examples of cities and industries are certainly sufficient to give the reader a good general idea on the business. Let us now consider the Manufactures of the United States as a whole, remembering that all calculations are based on the same system as the example of the New York Clothing factories, statement of which has been given. Here are the startling figures of the entire Manufacturing business of the United States for 1890:

Capital invested, $6,524,475,305.
Value of all manufactured products.....................$9,370,107,624
Miscellaneous expenses............$ 630,944,058
Wages paid................................. 2,282,823,265
Cost of materials used............... 5,158,868,353   8,072,635,676

Net profit..$1,297,471,948
Per cent of net profit on Capital for one year, 20.

This remainder shows the net profit on the capital invested in Manufactures. On 6500 millions of capital there are net profits of 1300 millions, or 20 per cent. This net profit, however, is subject to one further reduction. In each bulletin the Superintendent of Census says; "Expenses of selling are excluded, because the reported value of product is its selling value at the shop or factory." Hence, on the basis of the value given, it is proper to exclude any expenses or commissions for selling. But there is another item, of which the Superintendent says: "The cost of depreciation of plant in excess of the expense for ordinary repairs is not included, because the information obtained by the inquiry is not sufficient to form a basis for accurate computation for the respective industries." And yet, every one will concede that something should be deducted. Buildings wear out, and machinery more rapidly. This natural decay goes on in addition to the ordinary annual wear and tear. We may bestow a considerable sum each year to provide for ordinary repairs, occasioned by wear and tear, breakage, or otherwise. Still the immutable law of decay is going on, and a time must be reached when the structure must be rebuilt and the machinery replaced. In buildings this decay is less rapid than in machinery. The capital invested in Manufacturing Plants is in round numbers, 3239 million dollars, divided thus: land, 776 millions; buildings, 879 millions; machinery, tools and implements, 1584 millions.

What shall be our judgment as to the annual percentage of depreciation of these classes of property by reason of natural decay? The life of a building is long—perhaps sufficiently long that one or two per cent will be ample to provide compensation for this natural decay, in addition to the annual ordinary repairs. It is believed that no one will gainsay this proposition: that the increasing value of the land forming a part of the plant, by reason of the constantly growing density of population—that is to say, "the unearned increment"—is much greater than the losses to the buildings by reason of the natural decay.

The only difficulty we have to consider is as to the proper allowance to be made by reason of this natural decay to the machinery. And on this question the writer appeals to a judgment far superior to his own.

Mr. Lee Johnson, Kansas City, Kansas, Grand President of the Brotherhood of Boiler Makers and Iron Ship Builders of America, a man of large experience in machinery and ripe judgment in matters pertaining thereto, in response to an inquiry from the writer has kindly given his estimate, under date of March 31, 1894, and authorized its publication as follows:

"To answer your question with absolute correctness is impossible. However, an approximate average may be made which, if not correct, will not be far from it. The life of manufacturing machinery is estimated to be from 8 to 25 years, according to usage and class of machinery. This shows an average life of about 16½ years, and will make the depreciation or decay about

6 per cent per annum of the original total cost. This does not include repairs, which, in manufacturing machinery, equals from 4 to 5 per cent per annum of the original cost, also. In the motive power department of railroads, the 'wear and tear' of machinery is much greater, possibly averaging from 8 to 10 per cent per annum of the total cost, while the overhauling and general repairs on locomotives will equal from 9 to 12 per cent per annum of their original cost. The difference in the 'decay' or 'wear' between manufacturing machinery and railroad machinery is very marked. I believe the above is a conservative estimate in view of the limited statistics on the subject."

It is manufacturing machinery, not railroad machinery, that is considered here. This, Mr. Johnson says, will depreciate—will wear out—at the rate of 6 per cent per annum in addition to the amount expended yearly for ordinary repairs. Ordinary repairs are already deducted from the gross earnings. We have only the "natural decay" to provide for, and this, Mr. Johnson says, is 6 per cent each year. This will amount to 77 millions, leaving 1220 millions as the absolute net profit on the manufacturing capital of the country.

In nearly all the bulletins pertaining to the industries of the cities, Superintendent Porter congratulates the country on the increase in the wages of Labor. On this he says:

"Part of this increase is undoubtedly due to the fact that in many industries relatively more men were employed in 1890 and less children; that the percentage of increase in the number of women employed has been less in many industries than in the number of adult males; and also to the fact that in 10 years many branches of industry have improved the grades of their products, and for this reason require more skilled and higher paid employes. After making all possible allowances for these changes, for the more thorough enumeration for 1890, and for the advance in quantity of manufactured products, we have a decided relative increase in the amount paid in wages between 1880 and 1890."

Upon these facts Labor should receive the earnest congratulations of every friend of mankind. Wages have been increased, not by the voluntary action of Capital. Whatever has been accomplished is due to the well-directed efforts of Labor Organizations. And the measure of good that shall hereafter be achieved in this direction will depend on the more thoroughly united efforts of these Organizations. But the chief glory that clusters around the brow of Labor is in the first cause for the improvement assigned by the Superintendent—the decrease of child labor. This is one of the great reforms demanded, and now happily giving promise of accomplishment. While the number of all laborers has increased 66 per cent, the number of children employed has decreased 33 per cent, falling from 181,921 to 121,194. This is a noted success for Labor reform. Children belong in the schools of the country, not in the mines, shops and factories. The hope of the Nation is in their maturer education and intelligence.

The increase of wages, according to the Census Bulletin we are considering, between 1880 and 1890 was 38 per cent. In the former year the average earnings of the average laborer were $348 and in 1890, $481, showing a relative gain of 38 per cent. That is, the average earnings for the average number of laborers were $481. The average laborer who *worked all the time* was able to earn this amount. The reader must not lose sight of this fact. Every laborer was not able to earn this amount. He could only earn it by working *all* the time, and as many industries gave employment *part* of the time to many more laborers than could be used *all* the time, his earnings were so much less than this average as his time employed was less than the whole time. And this must be borne in mind in every instance where the earnings of 1890 are spoken of in this work.

But, if Labor gained in wages, how was it with the Producer in prices? Manufactured products increased so much in volume that their value grew from 5249 million dollars to 9054 millions, an increase of 69 per cent. How was it with raw materials? No one will deny that the raw materials, increasing in volume, should increase in value as much as the manufactured product, at least. Indeed, it must be admitted that they should increase in value more, because as the volume of business increases the less the margin of profit may be made. The difference between the raw materials and the manufactured products should be less in the larger business than in the smaller.

We find in examining this official bulletin that while the finished products increased in value 3805 millions, or 69 per cent, raw materials grew in value from 3395 millions to 5018 millions, an increase of 1623 million dollars, or 47 per cent.

Why did not the price of raw materials increase as much as the value of manufactured products? They should have advanced as much, at least.

Capital was compelled to advance the wages of Labor. It did so, but how? Simply by taking the increase of wages from the Producer. Raw materials should have shown an increase in value of 69 per cent in order to have shown fair treatment with the manufactured products. They should have grown from a total value of 3395 millions in 1880 to 5738 millions in 1890. But they grew to only 5018 millions, falling behind the manfactured products in relative gain 720 million dollars. It was of this sum the Manufacturing Enterprises wronged the Producers, yielding part of the booty by compulsion to the Laborers and keeping part themselves, being thus enabled to accumulate 20 per cent net profit per annum.

And this system of economics goes on and on in a sublime sweep of never-ending rythmic flow, while the hungry multitudes shout for the heroes that would "drain their sweat and drink their blood!" What a pretty thing it is! One great party in favor of "Tariff for revenue only," and the other great party in favor of "Only tariff for revenue." One great party in favor of knocking "protection" from under the Democratic sugar producers of the South, and the other retaliating with free trade for the Republican wool growers of the North. And now, finally, after many years of sham battles on false issues, one party demanding higher tariff on manufactured goods so that the Manufacturer may sell dearer and make greater profits; the other demanding free trade in raw materials in order that he may buy cheaper and make larger profits. They both arrive at the same goal—increased profits for the Manufacturer. The one theory is to rob the Consumer by too high prices and the other to rob the Producer by too low prices—all in the interest of Capital.

So long as the country shall adhere to the tariff idea, there can be no greater wrong upon the Producer than this idea of free raw materials. The Farmer who takes a hide to town and trades it for a hitch strap, should get a very good idea of the beauties of protected leather which he buys and free hide which he sells. Or, taking the clip of half a dozen sheep to town and trading it at the store for cloth enough to make a pair of trousers, should see the beauties of protection as applied to woolen goods which he buys and free trade as applied to the wool which he sells.

The poor tramp was not to blame, who, hired by the Farmer to shear sheep began at the tail rather than the head, and explained the innovation by assuring his employer of his inability to look an honest sheep in the face since he voted for the present administration and 10 cent wool. But this work is not a tariff treatise—that is, only "incidentally." But if tariff must come, in the name of justice to the Producers, let them have some benefits, and not strain every nerve to give all the profits to Manufacturers.

Gentlemen talk of the ill success of Manufacturers since the Census year. In reading these statements of the fabulous profits made by this greatest branch of American industry, defenders of the system will tell us we should show the losses of 1893 as well as the gains of 1890. This of course cannot be done, there being no data to govern such inquiry. Manufacturers have doubtless found less remunerative business since 1890 than prior thereto. In the nature of things this must be true. A long series of systematic plundering of the people under the guise of "Protecting American Labor" bore legitimate fruit. A time necessarily must come when the people could stand it no longer. The lemon squeezed dry must cease to yield its juices—the people robbed of all must cease to yield more money. Products of the factory could not be sold because the people could not buy. This fact was a very good reason for many enterprises to shut down. And then an object lesson. They believed they could shut down temporarily and assign the cause thereof to fears of threatened tariff reduction. And so they scared weak-minded Farmers, unthinking Laborers and overreaching Tradesmen into the belief that the country would go to utter moral and financial ruin unless its high standard could be maintained by a perpetuation of the robber system.

But why discuss this phase of the question further? The reader has seen that from the actual statistics of the Government, taken in the most careful and elaborate manner possible, and infinitely more complete than any other Census has been, the Manufacturers of the United States with 6½ billions of capital (less than one-ninth of the entire wealth of the country), accumulated 1220 million dollars of net profit (three-fifths of the entire wealth-gain of the country.)

Remember, the wealth-gain over the entire country was only 4½ per cent per year. Allowing the Manufacturers double the average increase they should have accumulated only 585 millions, instead of 1220 millions, a loss to the productive industries of the country of 635 million dollars. Is not that enough to satisfy any greed? But the politicians who seek to perpetuate these things tell you

>Digest things rightly
>Touching the weal o' the common, you shall find
>No public benefit which you receive
>But it proceeds or comes from them to you
>And no way from yourselves.

CHAPTER VI.

SOME VOCATIONS THAT DO NOT CONCENTRATE.

We have seen in the preceding Chapters some of the methods for the concentration of Wealth in the hands of the few. In this Chapter it may be profitable as well as interesting to consider some of the vocations from which no concentration flows. There are favored enterprises that reap where they have not sown, while others sow where they now have but little hope of reaping. The great heart of the toiling millions of the Nation is heavy with discouragement and doubt.

It is not the purpose of the writer to array one class of citizens against another class, or one section of the country against another section. If he can show to the toiling producer that he is deprived of the true meed of his labor and inspire him that is down to rise with better government, building up the broken places, the object of this work will be accomplished.

In order to set clearly before the mind some of the evils of the present economic conditions, a series of contrasts will be presented. The following Iowa object lesson will serve a good purpose:

"LOOK HERE,

UPON THIS PICTURE, AND ON THIS."

HORACE BOIES, LATE DEMOCRATIC GOVERNOR OF IOWA, IN HIS GREAT SPEECH IN NEW YORK, DECEMBER, 1890:

Statistics show that the average wages of able-bodied men upon the farms of Iowa are $18.50 per month, or about 70 cents per day and board, the lowest price paid any class of like laborers in the state; and yet out of 900 farmers reporting to our Commissioner of Labor Statistics during the present year, more than 800 claim this help at these wages has been employed at a loss, instead of a profit during each of the five years last past.

Out of the same number an equal portion assert that the actual cost of producing a corn crop, the most profitable of all that are raised within the state, has, during the same period, exceeded the entire value of the crop when harvested, saying nothing whatever of income from the capital invested in the land required to produce it.

It is estimated by those making these reports that the cost of producing an acre of corn ready for market is $8.00; that the average crop for five years has been 33 bushels, and statistics show that the average price of this corn in our local markets soon after harvest, during such period, has been 22 cents per bushel, making the entire value of the crop when marketed, $7.33, or 67 cents less than the actual cost of production at market rates of labor. What is true of the production of corn in Iowa is equally true of all the great staples raised on her farms.

It is, however, if we stop to reflect, easy to discern that if the chief business of a country is being done at a loss, and that the country is becoming rich, there must be some flagrant error in the industrial system that produces such a result.

I do not hesitate to say there is no possible justification for a system of laws that produces such a result.

It is infinitely better that this Nation should remain poor, with its property, such as it has, distributed among all its classes, than become the richest on the globe with its wealth concentrated in the hands of a few.

WILLIAM LARRABEE, LATE REPUBLICAN GOVERNOR OF IOWA, IN HIS GREAT WORK ON THE RAILROAD QUESTION:

Stock and bond inflation, it may confidently be asserted, has created from five to six thousand millions of dollars of fictitious railroad capital. In 1890 the average liabilities of the railroads of the United States, including capital stock and the funded and unfunded debt, were $63,600 per mile. According to Mr. Poor's estimate of the average cost of American railroads per mile, more than 50 per cent of this vast sum is pure water.

It is safe to say that $25,000 is a liberal estimate of the average cost per mile of American roads to the stock and bondholders, and that their capitalization represents $38,000 of water per mile. The total net earnings of the railroads of the country were $341,666,639 in 1890, and $356,227,883 in 1891, upon an actual investment of only about $4,225,000,000. This is a return of about 8½ per cent, and shows the force of Mr. Poor's statement that, if the water was squeezed out of railroad securities, no better paying investment could be found in the country.

We often see reference to the fact that no dividends are paid upon a large portion of railroad stocks, but there is no reason why dividends should be paid upon many of them, as they represent no capital whatever that has gone into the road.

It is probable that not to exceed ten cents on the dollar on the average was originally paid for these stocks, and the $80,000,000 distributed annually as dividends upon them does not vary much from 15 to 25 per cent upon the amount actually invested in them.

Gross earnings of Iowa railroads for year ending June, 1889, $37,469,376. For 1890, $41,318,133. For 1891, $43,102,399. For 1892, $44,540,000. The net earnings per mile of the Iowa roads were $1,421.91 in the year 1888-89, and $1,821.37 the year following. The total net earnings of all Iowa roads during the year ending June 30th, 1891, were $14,463,106, against $11,867,310, during the year ending June 30th, 1889, and were still greater for the year ending June 30th, 1892.

Here we have the testimony of a most highly respected citizen and honored Governor of the great agricultural state of Iowa, showing that farming is unprofitable in that most fertile of states. And he speaks not as one unadvised, for Governor Boies is one of the large farmers of the State. Agriculture, that has made Iowa great, is unprofitable—done at an actual loss in addition to the loss of all returns on the capital invested.

Another respected citizen and honored Governor gives his testimony on the railroad question. Governor Larrabee has been an extensive shipper, railroad director, president and manager. He knows whereof he speaks. And knowing he tells us that, for all the Union, railroads pay 8½ per cent net returns after paying all expenses, repairs, improvements, fancy salaries, taxes, etc. That the Iowa roads paid over $1800 per mile net profits when farms were being conducted at a loss. Iowa roads, built on her extensive prairies, are perhaps built at as little cost as any in the Union. And yet these net earnings, capitalized on the basis of five per cent net, pay fair returns on $36,000 per mile—perhaps fully three times the present cost of building such roads. Is not the contrast sufficiently marked? Does not the Iowa Farmer sow while the Railroad owner reaps?

Another contrast. This one shall be a Kansas contrast. It is very well known that Kansas Farmers who have fed stock the past decade have not been very prosperous—not many of them. Some have simply kept even. A few have made a profit, and many have failed. On the whole the business has not been profitable. It is even better known than the other proposition that laborers who have worked the raw material of live stock into the manufactured article of dressed or cured meats, have not been able to save anything. Where are the profits?

There are located at the mouth of the Kansas river in Kansas many large meat packing establishments. For 1890 the Census reports (see Bulletin No. 307) record the operations of these six large packing houses thus:

Capital invested, $8,964,586.
Aggregate value of manufactured products......................$39,927,191
Wages paid...$ 2,558,526
Principal materials used........................... 31,981,115
Fuel 132,598
All other materials.................................. 170,410
Taxes... 33,545
Insurance... 93,544
Repairs on buildings and machinery....... 70,605
Interest on cash used in the business...... 81,651
All sundries not elsewhere reported......... 3,150,795   38,272,789

Net Profit...$ 1,654,402
Percentage of net profit on capital, 18.

Observe, 18 per cent net profit, after paying every possible expense that can by any course of reasoning be deducted. Taxes are paid and insurance. Repairs are made and paid for out of gross earnings. But look! "Interest on cash used in the business," is paid from gross earnings. And to cover all possible accidents, they put down the astounding sum of $3,150,795 as

"Sundries not elsewhere reported." And yet after all this they cannot help showing more than 18 per cent net profit!

"All Sundries not elsewhere reported!" This is a most wonderful statement, in view of the enormous sum. A comparatively small item can be stated, with the purpose for which it was used. Fuel, Taxes, Insurance, Repairs, are but trifles compared with this magnificent sum of "Sundries." What is it? When in the common businesses of life an agent spends money for illegitimate purposes, he invariably calls it "Sundries," for want of a better name. What does "Sundries" mean here? Is it a vast corruption fund in order to perpetuate the present wrongs, or is it a part of the profits withdrawn from the business in order to deceive the public, or is it both of these and several more? *

Taxes, $33,545! Does the reader realize what this means? It is simply $3.74 on each $1,000 of actual value, for State, County, City, School District—every class of taxes levied. Think of it! On each $100 of actual value these great concerns that clear 18 per cent net, pay 37 cents taxes! How is it with the Laborer in these great concerns? As a general rule he is not bothered with taxes. But if, by some peculiar stroke

---

* If these "Sundries not elsewhere reported" were added to the net earnings the profit on capital for the one year would be about 54 per cent, instead of 18. As the writer has reliable private information to the effect that one of these concerns, and not the most profitable one, cleared 40 per cent net in 1893, he is inclined to think the net profit in 1890 should include the "Sundries."

of fortune, he should in some way become possessed of a humble little home worth, say $1,000, he will be required to pay taxes of not less than $20. Six times as much as the wealthy Manufacturer pays! And why? This low rate of tax for the Kansas City Packers is not exceptional. It is far above the average taxes on the reported industries of the cities named in Chapter V.

But how fare the Laborers in these great enterprises? There are employed an average of 4,617 persons. These are nearly all men, there being only 126 women and children reported. No one will think for a moment that this army of workmen have accumulated any wealth. Their average annual earnings are seen to be $554.* These Laborers, as a rule, have families to support. After paying rents, food, fuel, clothing, car fares and the multitude of "All Sundries not elsewhere reported," there can be but little left to lay up for the future. Indeed, it is safe to say there is nothing laid up. And why not? Why should not the labor of these men count for something? Why should not manhood and muscle be capitalized on a paying basis, and be allowed to accumulate something over operating expenses? In

---

* The average number of Laborers in 1890 was 4,617—sometimes much more and sometimes much less. A much larger number was employed. But the much larger number was not able to find employment *all the time*—only part time. And the much larger number, working *part of the time* was equal to 4,617 working *all the time*. Therefore, while the average earnings were $554 for *all the time*, they were really as much less as the time actually worked was less than full time.

olden times a negro slave possessed a commercial value of $1,000. Have we so degenerated that a white Laborer is less valuable than the former colored slave? To rate him no higher, the capital these Laborers possess in their muscle is worth $4,617,000. That capital ought to bring in its proportionate share of the net profits, even on the very degraded commercial basis mentioned. But in truth and fact they should do more than that. They should at least have half the profits. It is no good to say men spend their wages for liquor and riotous living. Unfortunately some do this. But in so doing they simply take so much from their lives, and must subsist that much the meaner. Not a man gets wages that he can afford to spend for dissipation, or from which he can hope to save any considerable sum. It is only such wages as he should spend in a decent support of himself and those dependent upon him. And living decently he will spend it all. If he spends less than all, he simply consents to live that much cheaper than any member of the free Republic should be required to live.

Let us take another example. This shall be from Philadelphia, the city of brotherly love. Everything should be fair and equitable there. Her 8 Sugar Refineries are reported thus for the operations of one year ending in 1890:

Capital invested, $8,207,655 (of which $1,095,000 is hired property.)
Aggregate value of manufactured product.......................$46,598,524

Wages paid..$	753,386	
Principal materials used...........................	41,141,841	
Fuel..	426,516	
Mill supplies..	6,977	
All other materials..................................	260,231	
Rent	76,722	
Taxes...	28,279	
Insurance..	43,807	
Repairs of buildings and machinery........	37,757	
Interest on cash used in business............	48,834	
All sundries not elsewhere reported.........	349,493	43,173,843

Net profit..$ 3,424,681
Percentage of net profit on capital, (other than hired property which received its payment in rent) 48.

The tax charges here are a little less than in the Kansas City case, this being under 35 cents per $100 of actual value. Considerably more conservative than the Kansas City packers in "Sundries not elsewhere reported,", turning over to that mysterious fund only about one-tenth as much. But the labor! Think of it, ye toilers! Paid for labor, $753,386; paid this sum to 1,519 men and 1,664 women, an average of $236 for each person! How much did they earn above "operating expenses?" And the capitalists who compel them to work for starvation wages clear a profit of more than three million dollars! Do you like the picture?

We have in these two examples as good illustration of the relations between Capital and Labor as we can find. In the one case it is a Western concern showing profits far below the average of great Manufacturing concerns, and showing the rate of wages far above the average. The other is an Eastern concern showing the highest profits of any of the great enterprises, and at the same time showing the lowest wages. These examples are surely enough to point a moral or adorn a tale. In order, however, that the reader may know that no deception is sought, mention is here made of several other enterprises, figuring in just the same manner, and whose profits for one year are shown below (in each case omitting the Hired Property which receives rent from gross earnings):

Census Bulletin No. 222, shows 186 Clothing Factories in Chicago, with over 12 millions of capital, (employing 6,727 hands whose annual earnings are $438), whose net profit is 46 per cent. 212 Foundries with 22 millions of capital employ 12,995 hands who average $593 per year; net profit, 31 per cent. 157 Furniture Factories with over 8 millions of capital work 8,295 hands who earn $574 each, and make 31 per cent net profit.

Bulletin No. 211 relates to New York. There 1554 Clothing Factories with nearly 30 millions of capital employ 37,811 hands who average $597 per annum; net profit, 37 per cent. 740 Women's Clothing Factories with over 10 millions of capital give work to 24,712 hands whose average annual earnings are $514 and capital earns 63 per cent net.

Bulletin No. 219 shows 323 Boot and Shoe Factories

in Lynn, Mass., employing nearly 8 millions of capital and 12,616 hands, who average $533 annual earnings and make a net profit for their employers of 40 per cent.

Bulletin No. 244 relates to Philadelphia where 717 Manufactories of Textile Fabrics with 66 millions of capital give employment to 57,414 hands whose average earnings are $373 per annum, and 22 per cent net profit is realized on the capital invested.

Bulletin No. 232, Boston. There 191 Clothing Factories with over 10 millions of capital employ 6,528 hands at an average wage of $507 per annum, and make 28 per cent on the capital.

Bulletin No. 367 shows 90 Silk Factories in Patterson, New Jersey, with more than 12 millions of capital. They employ 11,596 hands who average $433 annually, and return their employers 27 per cent net profit.

These examples are all taken at random, the only purpose being to select the largest industries. These concerns deducted less "Sundries not elsewhere reported" than the Kansas City Packers. Hence the profits of the packers *appear* more modest.

"Plate sin with gold, and the strong lance of Justice hurtless breaks." A Carnagie, a Rockafeller, an Armour may wrong the toiler and the producer, and from the price of their iniquity give a library, endow a college, or found a church. The pious throng will bless the hand that gives, never once thinking of the wronged laborer or producer who has been robbed in order that the millionaire may bring his rich gift to God. And then, perhaps, God gives the credit where it belongs. Who knows?

CHAPTER VII.

SOME RURAL SCENES WITHOUT CONCENTRATION.

It is believed that the attentive reader who has carefully followed these pages thus far is beginning to form a very good general idea of the entire and immeasurable injustice which the lesser number of people and the lesser amount of wealth have done the greater number of people and the greater amount of wealth. We have seen the great Concentration of Wealth into favored sections and favored classes. We have seen the Railroad owners, Bankers and Manufacturers taking to themselves three or four times their just and equitable reward. We have seen the frightful comparison of the rewards of Labor with the rewards of Capital. All these things have been startling to the student of economic questions, who was already well advanced in the unwelcome truths herein presented. If startling to such an one, how utterly overwhelming they must be to the novitiate who has carelessly drifted with the current, believing that something was wrong, but scarcely enquiring what, until he now seeks to find the difficulty.

It has been admitted in the preceding chapter that the wages of Labor advanced during the decade of which this is written. What of it? The average earnings of the average Laborer in the United States *who worked all the time* in 1890 were $481. It certainly was no more than he was entitled to, and most surely not more than enough to support himself and those dependent upon him. No statesman should dare to rejoice for one moment in the thought that American Labor in 1890 could earn $481, and that this was an advance over former years. He should blush to think that wages were ever less than that. It required every dollar of it to support Labor even in meager decency. If it ever was required to subsist on less, the blush of burning shame should be as the mark of Cain on the face of every law-maker who was responsible for the infamy. If it has advanced a little it has simply come that much nearer to its own, and come through its own efforts which forced recognition of its just claims.

Let us take a look at some rural scenes from the Census. In discussing the relative number of home-owners and the homeless in 1890 as compared with 1880, it is unfortunate that no inquiry was made in 1880 relative to the Laborers. So we cannot know what portion of that class of our citizens owned their homes and what portion rented. But with Farmers it is different. In their case owners and renters were counted both years. And from these counts the student of economic questions is able to draw a valuable lesson. What a beautiful harmony there is in all these startling facts! How nicely each will line up against every other! How perfectly every one will dovetail with all the others!

The entire count of farm-owning and farm-renting families for 1890 has not yet been completed. But Mr. Geo. K. Holmes, special agent in charge of that department of the Census, has furnished some careful computations in the article quoted from in the second chapter. His statement is based on the actual count in 22 states, and careful estimates as to the others. From his figures in connection with Census Bulletins, we glean another fact. And, remember, his estimate would not seek to favor the view here taken, but rather to oppose it. Look at these comparisons:

Entire population of the whole country increased 25 per cent.

Rural population (all outside of cities of 8,000 and over) increased 14 per cent.

Urban population (in cities of 8,000 and over) increased 61 per cent.

Entire number of farm families increased 9½ per cent.

Farm-owning families increased 2½ per cent.

Farm-renting families increased 40½ per cent. *

There is the picture! Look at it, you miserable political hucksters trafficking in the lives, liberties and homes

---

* If the reader cares for the exact figures, he has them here. Total population increased from 50,155,783 to 62,622,250, a gain of 12,466,467, or 25 per cent. Rural population increased from 38,837,236 to 44,286,580, a gain of 5,449,344, or 14 per cent. Urban popu-

of your people! You have driven the independent home-owning people of this country, in unnumbered legions, from country to over-crowded city—from prosperous owners to struggling tenants.

Mr. Carroll D. Wright, Labor Commissioner, now in charge of the Census Bureau, says in Extra Bulletin No. 63, issued last December, that the source for the statistics for 1880 and 1890 are not the same, since the figures for 1880 represents farms and those for 1890 farm families, and this may somewhat affect the comparison. Then he shows that the number of owned farms in the 22 states and territories considered had increased 1 per cent and the hired farms increased 49 per cent. In the Southern and Eastern states the number of owned farms actually decreased. A majority of the 22 states and territories considered (Arizona, Connecticut, District of Columbia, Georgia, Idaho, Iowa, Maine, Maryland, Massachusetts, Minnesota, Montana, Nevada, New Hampshire, New Jersey, New Mexico, Rhode Island, South Carolina, Tennessee, Utah, Vermont, Wisconsin and Wyoming), show an actual decrease of farm-owning families that is frightful, and while taken as a whole the increase is only 1 per cent. It takes the rapidly increasing population of Arizona, Idaho, Montana, New

---

lation increased from 11,318,547 to 18,235,670, a gain of 6,917,123, or 61 per cent. Farm families increased from 4,008,907 to 4,500,000, a gain of 491,093, or 9½ per cent. Farm-owning families increased from 2,984,306 to 3,060,000, a gain of 75,694, or 2½ per cent. Farm-renting families increased from 1,024,601 to 1,440,000, a gain of 415,399, or 40½ per cent.

Mexico, Utah and Wyoming, to be added to the older states in order to show even one per cent in farm-owning families. All the states and territories named above gained largely in tenant farmers. Even the great Middle West that feeds the world, and the Sunny South that blesses all with fruits and flowers, are degrading their landed proprietors to humiliating tenantry. Look at these figures and blush: From 1880 to 1890 Georgia tenant Farmers increased from 62,175 to 102,081; Iowa from 44,174 to 60,737; Minnesota from 8,453 to 17,982; South Carolina from 47,219 to 72,187; Tennessee from 57,196 to 76,949; Wisconsin from 12,159 to 19,436. Are we not fast becoming a land of paupers?

Western and Southern farmers must not think that they suffer alone. It makes no difference where it is—the picturesque fields of New England, the bottomless soils of the Middle West, the cotton plantations and orange groves of the South, the wheat farms of the great Northwest, the fruit fields of the Pacific, or the pastoral hills and dales of the North, all are under the ban of the tyranical Money Power that is carrying every industry but its own to certain destruction. The writer has many times pronounced his strictures on the the North Atlantic states, and condemned the course pursued by those states in their action on economic questions. He will continue to condemn their political action as long as the suffering people there will permit their political prostitutes to bind them hand and foot without protest. At the same time he has tried to be understood as excepting the suffering people there from any charge of intended wrong. Their error is in permitting the wrongs to be inflicted. They haven't thought enough for themselves. They have blindly gone on voting as the bosses have directed, never thinking they were bargaining away their birth-right cheaper than Esau did. But the good and suffering people of the East should know that "Evil is wrought by want of thought as well as want of heart."

The writer has long been aware that while the Money Power of New England has been drawing to those states ten times their share of the wealth of the country, yet that New England had her share of the distress of paupers, convicts, youthful offenders, and impoverished Laborers and Farmers, all produced, not by any inherent weakness or vice in the unfortunate people, but forced upon them by infamously unjust laws. Why the oppressed people who endure the hardships there do not hurl their oppressors from power is one of those mysteries reserved for Omniscience.

In order that the Northern, Southern and Western Farmer may see how his suffering brethren fare in the extreme East, and in order that the brethren themselves may understand their condition more fully, an object lesson is here given from Extra Bulletin No. 63. Look at it. This is of the six New England states.

SEED TIME OF THE FARMERS.

Number of owned farms, 1880	189,572
Number of farm-owning families, 1890	165,455
Decrease, 15 per cent	24,117
Number of hired farms, 1880	17,660
Number of farm-hiring families, 1890	24,906
Increase, 41 per cent	7,246

Thus her home-owners were made homeless in 10 years to the extent of 24,117. What became of these 24 thousand homes? They did not all pass into the hands of tenants, because we find only 7,246 increase there. Here are 16,871 farm homes unaccounted for. Where are they? Either abandoned or consolidated with other farms, pleasing to the fancy of some city Capitalist who wants to revel in the luxury of a large estate, in harmony with the habits of his European model. When will New England wake and shake off the horrid incubus?

The reader will doubtless be interested in some specimen profits on farming. We have seen the profits of other enterprises. Let us look at the net returns from farming, making no item of "All sundries not elsewhere reported." At a recent meeting of the Cecil, Maryland, Farmers' Club, Mr. Thomas C. Bond presented some figures on the cost of production of grain. His statements there seemed to have met the endorsement of the Club, and have attracted considerable attention. It is believed Mr. Bond is conservative in his statement. His estimated cost of producing 10 acres of wheat in Maryland on basis of hiring all labor at market rates (which is the basis in each of the following statements) was as follows:

Cost of plowing 10 acres, 1 team 6 days at $3	$ 18.00
Cost of first harrowing, 1 team 1½ days	4.50
Cost of second harrowing, 1 team 1½ days	4.50
Cost of rolling, 1 team 1½ days	4.50
20 bushels of seed at 75 cents	15.00
Drilling wheat, 1 team 1½ days	4.50
One man tending drill 1½ days	1.50
Cutting wheat with binder, 1½ days at $5	7.50
2 men to set up wheat, 1½ days at $1.50	4.50
Man to drive reaper, 1½ days at $1	1.50
Team hauling in wheat, 2 days at $3	6.00
2 men loading and putting away, 2 days at $1.25	5.00
Cost of threshing, 200 bushels at 5 cents	10.00
4 men taking away straw, 1 day at $1.25	5.00
Hauling wheat to market, 1½ days at $3	4.50
Extra man, 1½ days at $1.25	1.88
2 tons of fertilizer at $28	56.00
Interest and insurance on buildings	70.00
Total cost for 10 acres	$224.38
Sold 200 bushels of wheat at 65 cents......$130.00	
Sold 10 tons of straw at $5.................. 50.00	180.00
Net loss	$ 44.38

It is difficult to be able to find much fault with this. If the critical reader should think that Mr. Bond is farming too expensively he must remember that Maryland lands require expensive farming. If there is too much fertilizer, remember he sells the straw; if too much other expenses on the one hand, notice the magnificent average yield, and the price *several cents above New York markets.*

That is an Eastern estimate. Having seen wheat growing on the Potomac, let us look at it on the Columbia. Mr. Nathan Pierce is one of the largest, most practical and conservative of the Farmers of the magnificent wheat country in Northeastern Oregon. He furnishes specially for this work a statement of operations on a section of the famous Umatilla lands as follows:

Cost of plowing 640 acres at $1.25,	$ 800
Cost of preparing for planting at 70 cents	448
Cost of planting and seed at 85 cents	544
Harvesting at $2.50 per acre	1600
Cost of marketing, average haul, at 2 cents	320
Taxes paid for 1893 and 1894 on farm	275
Insurance on buildings and grain	128
Ordinary repairs on house, fences, etc	175
Sacks and shipping charges	800
Interest on $16,000, 2 years at 10 per cent	3200
Total expenditure	$8290
Average crop, 25 bushels per acre, making a total yield of 16,000 bushels, worth in the local markets 34 cents	5440
Net loss	$2850

No one, it is believed, will quarrel with Mr. Pierce for excessive charges. However, it is desirable that his brethren not so far West should know something of wheat farming in far-off Oregon. Harvesting out there means cutting with the header, drawn either by an engine or some 20 horses, threshing, cleaning and sacking the wheat as it goes, laying it on the ground and leaving it there until the farmer is ready to haul to market. Taxes and Interest are charged for two years, because this crop is all that will be harvested for two years. In lieu of fertilizers the Oregon Farmer lets his land rest in summer fallow every alternate year, and the preparing for planting is in two harrowings given the ground while it rests, to kill the weeds. The bulk of the Insurance charged is on the grain in the fields before harvest. The reader will see that a combination of cutting, threshing and cleaning in one operation requires a very ripe harvest, which is not infrequently destroyed by great fires that sweep portions of the country.

Mr. Bond figures on Maryland corn-farming thus:

Plowing 10 acres, 6 days at $3	$ 18.00
First harrowing, 1½ days at $3	4.50
Second harrowing, 1½ days at $3	4.50
Rolling, 1¼ days at $3	3.75
Marking out, 2 days at $3	6.00
2 men planting, 2 days at $1	4.00
Covering, team 2 days at $2	4.00
Team first working, 4 days at $2	8.00
Team second working, 4 days at $2	8.00
Cutting, 800 shocks at 1½ cents	12.00
Husking, 800 shocks at 1½ cents	12.00
Hauling in, 1 team 3½ days at $3	10.50
Hauling in fodder, 2½ days at $3	7.50
2 men to put away fodder, 2½ days at $1	5.00
Shelling corn, 2 men 3 days at $1	6.00
Hauling to market	6.00
Seed corn	1.25
2 tons fertilizer at $28	56.00
Interest, and Insurance on buildings	70.00
Total cost of ten acres	$247.00

Yield 450 bushels of corn, at 50 cents..................$225.00
Yield 1600 bundles of fodder, at 3 cents............. 48.00   273.00
    Net profit..$ 26.00

Does Mr. Bond farm too expensively? Maryland requires expensive farming. But look at his yield—far above the average yield of any state in the Union for a series of years. His selling price is several cents above New York quotations. He is more than fair—enough beyond fair to more than wipe out the profit.

Mr. Geo. W. Beer is one of the best farmers in Fulton County, Illinois. He confidently believes that he lives in the best part of the best state in the Union, and probably cannot get up much discussion on that point. Not in harmony with the writer in his views on economic questions, he certainly is not prejudiced in favor of the position here taken. He has kindly furnished for this publication his estimate of the outlay and the income from corn culture in his section of the country, as follows:

Cost of plowing 100 acres..$ 150.00
  " preparing for planting... 25.00
  " planting, including seed.. 33.00
  " cultivating.. 250.00
  " gathering and cribbing crop... 150.00
  " marketing (average distance to haul)......................... 125.00
  " taxes on land for 1 year.. 40.00
  " ordinary repairs on fences, etc..................................... 37.00
  " Interest on $7,500, 1 year, 7 per cent........................ 525.00
    Total cost of 100 acres of corn...........................$1335.00
Yield, 4500 bushels of corn, at 27 cents................................ 1215.00
    Net loss..$ 120.00

Mr. Beer's estimate of yield seems high. It certainly is higher than the average yield for a series of years in his own great state. However, he is figuring on the best land—land reasonably worth $75 per acre—and therefore puts the yield above the average of his state or even his county for a series of years. If the reader should say that he allows nothing for fodder he must notice that he charges nothing for cutting it; if he allows nothing for fodder he must notice that he charges nothing for fertilizers, and even Illinois land will wear out in time if starved.

Mr. James K. Polk Barker is one of the thrifty and substantial farmers of Wyandotte County, Kansas, living about 5 miles from Kansas City. His part of the country is thus seen to be very favorably situated with reference to market. Although at the present more of a fruit farmer than a grain farmer, he is well posted from life-long experience with all the phases of land culture. He tells us the result on 100 acres of land in his neighborhood, one-half planted in corn and one-half in wheat, as follows:

Cost of plowing...$	125.00
" preparing for planting..	20.00
" planting 50 acres of corn and seed........................	15.00
" planting 50 acres of wheat...	10.00
" seed wheat...	30.00
" man and team 60 days cultivating corn..................	180.00
" gathering 1500 bushels of corn.................................	60.00
" harvesting wheat, $1.25 per acre..............................	62.50
" threshing 800 bushels wheat from shock...............	32.00

"	6 men and teams hauling to machine............	18.00
"	22 men one day at $1.50.........................	33.00
"	taxes for one year..............................	45.00
"	ordinary repairs on fences, etc.................	15.00
"	hauling to market, 1500 bushels corn at 5 cents......	75.00
"	hauling to market, 800 bushels of wheat at 5 cents,	40.00
Interest on $8,000 invested in farm, 8 per cent..............		640.00
	Total cost 50 acres corn and 50 acres wheat.....	$1,400.50
Yield, 1500 bushels of corn at 30 cents...............	$450.00	
"	800 bushels of wheat at 50 cents............. 400.00	850.00
	Net loss...	....$550.50

Mr. Barker credits nothing to the account for straw or fodder, nor charges anything for fertilizers. This should be a fair off-set. It is not probable that much has been omitted in the showing. If the reader thinks the yield is too small, he should take notice that it is considerably above the state average for the past ten years.

Texas furnishes an interesting example in Cotton culture in that great state. Mr. T. S. DeArmand of Nevarro County, writes: "I have placed the crop high, but our best farmers have made an average of a half bale per acre for the past ten years. I want to give full estimate. I have put the cultivation low. I give the price of cotton and seed, as seed is now a large item in the crop. I count 1600 pounds to make a bale of 500 pounds and pay the toll, including the bagging and ties." Here are Mr. DeArmand's figures on one acre of cotton culture:

Preparing ground for planting	$ 2.00
Planting and seed	.65
Cultivating	4.50
Gathering crop	6.00
Marketing (average distance to haul)	2.50
Rent of cotton land	4.00
Bagging and ties	.35
Cost of one acre of cotton	$20.00
Yield, one-half of 500 pound bale at 6½ cents...$16.25	
Seed from same... 2.50	18.75
Net loss on one acre of cotton	$ 1.25

It may be a matter of regret that Mr. DeArmand did not go more minutely into details. But he has evidently gone far enough to show that cotton culture based on the reasonable value of land and labor is not profitable at the current market rates of 6½ cents per pound. Good lands peculiarly adapted to the growing of cotton were the most highly valued lands before vicious financial legislation had destroyed the value of the crop. Now we can see that no more than reasonable wages need be expected. The Census reports for 1890 show the average yield of Texas to be 0.37 of a bale, while Mr. DeArmand's county, one of the most productive in the state, averaged 0.41. In 1880 the county average was less. So we can readily believe the yield given above to be large enough.

CHAPTER VIII.

NO CONCENTRATION FOR TRADESMEN.

The reader has seen in the preceding chapters the great gains that have resulted to Capital invested in Railroads, in Banks and in Manufactures. He is also well satisfied from his every day observations of the conditions surrounding him, and from a careful reading of the foregoing pages that the Laborers and Farmers of the land have not been accumulating wealth. There is another class that have suffered equally with the Laborers and Farmers. The Tradesmen of the land have been meeting their Waterloo as well as the others. They, too, have been doing business on a falling market in many of the staple goods they have handled, brought about by the contracted currency of the country. The blight is on all industries and all businesses, except those whose fabulous aggrandizement of wealth has become great enough to make laws for their protection, no matter what the cost to all others.

Whatever demand there may be for railroad legislation that should compel these great corporations to acknowledge themselves servants of the people in operating the great highways of the country's commerce, to the end that the producers may find a way to market at reasonable cost, railroad capital has been potent enough to defeat any proposed reforms. Whatever restrictive usury laws may have been demanded by the people regulating the rates of interest, or demanding a greater issue of money on which to transact the business of the country, enhance the value of all the products of industry, or cheapen the rates of interest to the borrower, the banking capital of the country has been strong enough to defeat desirable legislation, and scarce money, low prices and high interest continue to crush the people. Whatever pleas may have gone from the producers and consumers to their law-makers praying to be protected from the greed of combines and trusts that have been constantly forcing down the value of raw materials and forcing up the price of manufactured goods, there always has been an abundance of manufacturing capital ready for the work of protecting itself under the false pretence of protecting American Labor. The Laborers, Farmers and Tradesmen outnumber the Railroad owners, Bankers and Manufacturers as the poor have always outnumbered the rich. The vote of the weak is as effective as the vote of the strong, if the weak will only exercise it as wisely. "And must they all be hanged that swear and lie?" asks the precocious little Macduff. "Every one," his mother assures him. "Who must hang them?" "Why, the honest men."

"Then the liars and swearers are fools, for there are liars and swearers enow to beat the honest men and hang up them." But it is quite probable that the wicked men of the Macduff era were no more submissive to the honest men, than the poor people of to-day are to the rich. It was about the same measure of self-sacrifice in either case.

It was said that Tradesmen suffered from falling markets. And truly they did. But their chief suffering came from others who suffered first. Their suffering was chiefly a borrowed suffering, as the moon's light is a borrowed light. The Tradesman who bought a thousand overcoats to sell a thousand workmen was unable to meet his bills if by reason of non-employment only five hundred could buy. The thousand Sunday dresses for the workmen's wives, together with hats, bonnets, gloves, shoes and the myriad of other articles that find ready and profitable sales with good times and steady employment, are left on hand when Labor is idle, and the Tradesman suffers with the suffering of others. The grocer's sales to the Farmer and the merchant's sales to the Farmer's wife will be meager indeed if by reason of the low prices of farm products money must be borrowed to pay taxes on the farm and interest on the farm mortgage. When the merchant and grocer are no longer able to sell to the Farmer, they will begin to feel the stress of hard times that will soon lead to failure. And these failures of the retail Tradesmen will reach the wholesale dealer and he suffers with the rest. Finally the trouble reaches the Manufacturer. He does not fail. Why should he? A series of years of unparalleled profits has placed him in a position where he can be absolutely impervious to the distress of others. He simply stops his machinery, and, utterly regardless of their fate, discharges his employees, calmly folds his arms and waits for a revival of business when the people shall have partially recovered from the ten years extortion he has practiced on them. The choir then sings that soul-stirring anthem born of lofty statesmanship and self-sacrificing patriotism, commencing, "Tin! Tin! American tin!"

Carnegie thereupon makes a gloriously patriotic speech assuring the country that the greatest blessing that can possibly befall any nation is the accumulation of colossal fortunes in the hands of a few—the greater the fortune and the fewer the fortunate possessors, the better. Then all the people shout. Statesmen appeal to the voters to stand firmly by the ever glorious principles of their respective party, and march again to glory, power and honor under the " lily-white banner " of pure and unsullied Democracy or Republicanism as the case may be, and with no material difference which. And so another great victory is achieved, the spoils of office belong to the spoilsmen, and the people at large enter upon a four year's term of unresisting submission to the same system of public plunder that characterized the previous term.

Unfortunately, perhaps, the distress of Tradesmen

is not a subject of Census inquiry. The Superintendent has given us no information as to the number of business men whose homes and fortunes have been wrecked by the wicked financial policy that has been pursued. But The Bradstreet Company is considered in all matters pertaining to mercantile affairs to be entirely reliable. Having been engaged in commercial reporting for the past 40 years or more, they are very familiar with all the phases of financial panics.

Their record for 1893 shows some very startling figures. For the six years last past their record is as follows;

YEAR.	NO. FAILURES.	ASSETS.	LIABILITIES.
1888	10,587	$61,999,911	$120,242,402
1889	11,719	70,596,769	140,359,490
1890	10,673	92,775,625	175,032,836
1891	12,394	102,893,000	193,178,000
1892	10,270	54,774,106	108,595,248
1893	15,508	231,486,730	382,153,676

Does the reader admire the record? There has been no other year in the history of the country when the number of failures or the liabilities equaled the terrific business slaughter of 1893. It was the climax of the many years of property destruction that had preceded it.

The conspiracy of Capital has been going on for years. Its red hand and bloody eye has become the menace of all our industries. The Legislation it has bought has become the charnel house for the dead hopes of the people. Through its influence the circulating medium of the country has been contracted to the destruction of all values, except on all such commodities as monopolies, trusts and combines could control. Fancy salaries, controlled by Capital, have advanced enormously, while the articles of productive industry with which such salaries must be paid, have decreased in a greater degree. This thought can best be illustrated in comparing the salaries and prices that prevailed for a few years after the war with the salaries and prices now. Based on the average New York prices of the former period we can ascertain that great Lincoln's salary as President could be paid with the price of 10,000 bushels of wheat; or 20,000 bushels of corn; or 50,000 pounds of wool; or 1,000 barrels of mess pork; or 500 head of cows; or 125 horses. To pay Cleveland's salary would require the proceeds, based on the present New York markets, of 75,000 bushels of wheat; 110,000 bushels of corn; 500,000 pounds of wool; 4,000 barrels of mess pork; 2500 head of cows, or 625 horses. *

Or, to put this another way, if the articles whose values were required to pay Cleveland's salary had been sold at the prices of 30 years ago, they would have produced the following magnificent sums, which may be said to be Cleveland salaries. The wheat needed to pay Cleveland, if sold at the prices of 30 years

---

* The writer is indebted to Mr. I. E. Dean, of New York, for the idea and most of the figures in this illustration, in his plea to "Save the American Home."

ago, would have yielded $187,500; corn, $137,500; wool, $250,000; mess pork, $100,000; cows, $125,000; horses, $125,000. This is what Cleveland's salary amounts to paid in products at the prices of Lincoln's time. Lincoln's salary was $25,000. He was worth it to the people. Cleveland gets from 6 to 10 times as much, measured by the value of products. He is worth it—to the enemies of the people.

While this destruction of the people's interests has been going on, the Railroads have kept up their tariff rates, forcing the Producer to pay as high transportation charges as ever. The Bankers have charged as high usury as ever in all cases, and much higher as a general rule, forcing payments in four or five times the quantity of products that were formerly required. The Manufacturer has been shrieking for a higher tariff schedule in order that he may force up the value of manufactured products and force down the value of all necessary raw materials, his only desire being greater profits to himself, *for the protection of American plunderers*. And while all these evil and destructive practices have been going on, the Railroad owners, Bankers and Manufacturers have been systematically avoiding their just share of the burden of taxation, by the peculiar methods known best to themselves, and imposing the additional burden on those unable to bear it.

It is not strange that the climax has come at last. Indeed it is strange that it came not sooner. The grandest commentary on the greatness of this country is that the people have been able to exist at all, under all the systematic plundering that has been practiced on them. Reduced to poverty by a designing tyrannical Money Power, the American people have shown an astonishing vitality in living through their political disgrace and disease.

The producers, unable to buy the products they need because of the poverty to which they have been reduced, the dry goods merchant, the grocer, the clothier, and the tradesman generally, are driven to bankruptcy by reason of small sales. And these Tradesmen in turn distress their wholesale merchants who, in their turn, follow the retail dealer to financial ruin. And these failures in turn induce the Manufacturer *to shut down his plant* to await better times. His workman becomes idle, helpless, hopeless, moneyless. As a factor in commerce he ceases. Without money he cannot buy. Other dealers feel the loss of his trade and they fail. The country feels the general panic and all is utter chaos. These are the conditions in 1894, brought about by the greed of gain that has actuated the Money Power of the land in fashioning the legislation that has well-nigh ruined a once happy and prosperous people. And yet they have the hardihood to tell the people that Labor is idle because of threats to lighten the robber tariff that has done more than any other cause to curse the industries of the people. The Tradesmen must array themselves with the Producers and the Laborers if they hope for success. They will get no assistance from the Railroad owners, Bankers and Manufacturers. Unless they shall awaken to the danger that threatens all of the common people, and help in the reform of things wrong, it will not be long until they, too, will be hunting for work, and protesting their

"Hunger for bread, not thirst for revenge."

CHAPTER IX.

THE MORTGAGE CURSE AS A FACTOR IN CONCENTRATION.

Extra Census Bulletin No. 64 was issued last December by Mr. Carroll D. Wright, in charge of the Bureau. Some of its facts will doubtless be of interest to the reader, in view of the many publications in the newspapers that have been made on this subject, some correct, but generally erroneous. The statistics for this Bulletin were prepared by Mr. George K. Holmes, special agent of the Census Bureau for this purpose. The details of the mortgage indebtedness were taken by Census agents in 33 states and territories. Upon these details the Bureau estimates the debt for the remaining states and territories. We find in this official bulletin the following damaging facts:

The mortgage debt of the United States on the 1st of January, 1890, was 6 billion dollars. That terrific debt has grown in the 10 years 156 per cent. Does the reader comprehend that statement? Look at it in the light of other growths. Population increased 25 per cent;

wealth of the entire country increased 45 per cent; *the mortgage indebtedness of the people 156 per cent!*

Increase in population
Increase in wealth
Increase in mortgage debt

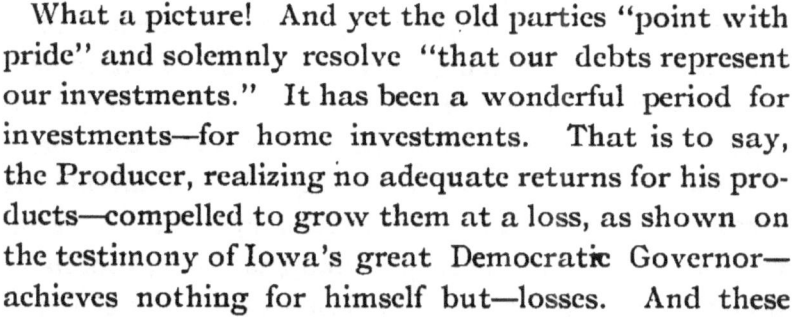

What a picture! And yet the old parties "point with pride" and solemnly resolve "that our debts represent our investments." It has been a wonderful period for investments—for home investments. That is to say, the Producer, realizing no adequate returns for his products—compelled to grow them at a loss, as shown on the testimony of Iowa's great Democratic Governor—achieves nothing for himself but—losses. And these losses he invests—invests in a mortgage on his home. And so the country prospers. The Producer has gained something. He simply had a home before. He has a home decorated with a mortgage now. He is gaining.

Do not think that the Farmer is hurt alone. Not by any means. The business man in the city who has invested his money in buildings with the hope of fair returns in rents; the mechanic or Laborer whose hard work and sacrificing economy in the years past enabled him to acquire a modest home; the Farmer who became the owner of a home by inheritance or homestead—it matters not where situated, by whom owned or how acquired, the breath of the blighting Upas of Monopoly is over them all. The curse of the oppressor is on the sweating brow of Industry. No city, town, village, or country district is exempt. This bulletin shows it. The people of the cities who belong not to the three great ruling and ruining classes suffer as much as the people of the country. A little over one-third (34 per cent) of the mortgage indebtedness existing January 1st, 1890, was on acre property, and a little less than two-thirds (66 per cent) was on lots. Therein is a hope. The people of the cities, who are now unable to rent their property for enough to pay taxes and make repairs, are beginning to realize that something is wrong. They are just rubbing their eyes after waking from a deep dream of peace to find that they, too, have been ruined by a policy that destroys all but the destroyer.

In previous lectures and essays the writer has tried to show that while the North Atlantic States are responsible for all the ills we suffer because the Railroad, Bank and Manufacturing despoilers of the Nation nearly all live within those states, yet that the masses of the people there are no more exempt from the general ruin than are the people of the other states. The per capita mortgage indebtedness of the several states will show the truth of this. The bulletin now under consideration gives the per capita of such debt for every man, woman and child residing in each of the several states. Here are those states owing $100 or more for each person: New York, $268; District of Columbia, $226; Colorado, $206; California, $200; Kansas, $170; Minnesota, $155; Massachusetts, $144; Nebraska,

HARVEST OF THE USURERS. 117

$126; Pennsylvania, $117; Connecticut, $107; Rhode Island, $106; Iowa, $104; Illinois, $100. This is the per capita debt for each man, woman and child as exhibited by the mortgage record. Estimating 5 persons for the average family, the reader can see the depth of the curse.

The compilers of Census Bulletin No. 64 say: "What the amount of existing real estate mortgage debt in the United States was in 1880 it is impossible to determine except roughly by a process of reasoning. In 1890, January 1st, the debt was about $6,000,000,000, one-sixth of this amount being an estimate for states not tabulated. As already pointed out, a progressive movement characterized the debt incurred during the decade under consideration, and, if it may be assumed that the life of mortgages and the proportion of partial payments have not changed materially from the beginning to the end of the decade, the following formula may be regarded as approximately sound: The debt incurred in 1889 is to the debt incurred in 1880 as the debt existing January 1, 1890, is to the debt existing January 1, 1880." By this formula Mr. Holmes concludes that the real estate mortgages existing in 1880 amounted to 2,343 million dollars, increasing in 10 years to 6000 millions, a gain of 3,657 million dollars, or 156 per cent! That ought to be quite sufficient to satisfy the most exacting and extreme greed of all the conspirators.

Real estate mortgages, $6,000,000,000! An increase

of $3,657,000,000! Per cent of increase, 156! Tenant Farmers, 1,440,000! An increase of 415,399! Per cent of increase, 40½! How long will it require for the Big Three to become the owners of all the land? How many years shall we wait until the tenant-farmers outnumber the farm-owning farmers? Then how long until all shall be tenants? These questions are all susceptible of mathematical demonstration. The day is coming for the accomplishment of all these things unless the people rouse from their lethargy.

When the conspirators took hold of matters it was necessary, in order to facilitate their work of spoliation, that new laws be passed for the collection of debts. Then it was that the several legislatures began to depart from the ancient landmarks, and find some new means for the speedy transfer of title by forced sale. It was formerly the practice that property exposed to forced sale should be appraised by disinterested persons thereto appointed by the court, and that it must be sold for not less than two-thirds or three-fourths of the appraised value, as the case may be. The conspirators did not want to pay so large a portion of the value as that. They knew the property must sooner or later fall into their hands, and they wanted to get it as cheaply as possible. It was then they began to get the laws amended. They wanted to be permitted to sell without appraisement. And so it was provided that when a debtor would put into his note or mortgage the words, "appraisement waived," or their equivalent, then in any judgment that may be rendered to enforce collection the real estate of the debtor may be sold without appraisement to the highest bidder, *at whatever price may be offered*. And there are those who justify that legalized robbery. They say the debtor need not make the waiver unless he wants to. Ah! but he must. He is compelled to borrow money. The lender says he must waive the appraisement, *and he must*. And so the waiver is put into the instrument, default is made in the payment, judgment is rendered, order of sale is issued, another advertisement of Sheriff's sale graces the local paper, the day of sale comes, the lender is on hand to bid just as little or just as much as he sees fit. As the Sheriff gets a commission on the selling price the larger the bid the more the cost. The cheaper the creditor buys it the less will be the cost to pay, and the more of judgment he will have left to keep hanging over the debtor awaiting further property in his hands. It is not an uncommon thing for the creditor to bid as small as one-tenth of the debt. If judgment was for $1,000 he may bid $100 for the land. Nobody else bids. The creditor buys it, the $100 bid by him is credited on the judgment, $900 is still left unpaid by virtue of which the creditor may levy on the personal property of the debtor, or may wait until he becomes possessed of some. The farm the man mortgaged for *one-third its value* is gone, and still the debt is unpaid.

When that celebrated money lender of Venice was the plaintiff in a foreclosure suit the judge said to him:

> This bond doth give thee here no jot of blood;
> The words expressly are "a pound of flesh:"
> Take then thy bond, take thou thy pound of flesh;
> But, in the cutting it, if thou dost shed
> One drop of Christian blood thy lands and goods
> Are, by the laws of Venice, confiscate
> Unto the state of Venice.

That was better law than our law of to-day. Or else it was a more equitable administration of the law by a more humane court. The judge of to-day is dangerously likely to say:

> I think this bond doth give thee flesh and blood,
> Although the words are writ "a pound of flesh."
> Take then thy bond, take thou thy pound of flesh;
> Take all he has and call it just a pound,
> And with it take the blood and hide and hair
> And watch his carcass till it grow thee more
> To satisfy thy wants.

The writer thinks that inasmuch as the mortgagee loaned his money four or five years ago on the basis that the farm or the lot was worth at least twice as much, generally three times as much, as the amount loaned, he ought now to be satisfied to take the farm for the debt, and square accounts. He should not be permitted to take the property and still hold a judgment against the debtor for a large unpaid balance to threaten and harrass him as long as he lives, finally driving him through discouragement to the grave. He should be satisfied with the "pound of flesh" that he contracted for. The Producers are not a dishonest set of people. They do not desire to avoid payment of their just obligations. They want to pay their debts and pay them according to the bond. They do not see, and now that they are waking from their long confiding slumber, they never will see, the justice of being compelled to pay their obligations in money two or three times dearer than they contracted. If when they borrowed it they could pay a thousand dollar debt with a thousand bushels of wheat, they do not believe it is just to take 2500 bushels for that purpose now; if 25 cows would pay the debt when they borrowed, they do not like to use 60 cows for that purpose now; if 6,000 pounds of cotton would pay the debt then, why be compelled to use 16,000 pounds now? It is very oppressive to the Farmer to see 15 horses sold to pay the debt now, when only 6 or 7 would have been necessary when he contracted the debt.

CHAPTER X.

THE CRIME AGAINST SILVER.

Of all the suicidal, ruinous and infamous legislation that has blasted and blighted this or any other nation the crime against silver is certainly one of the deepest. What was the cause that led to it? England many years prior to 1873 had demonetized silver, and had induced many other nations to follow her example. Her national life, builded on greed and blood, had made her the creditor nation of the earth. It was then she held in her capacious grasp the securities of the world. It would be eminently profitable for England, under those circumstances to increase the purchasing power of money—when the world held the production and she held the gold. Looked at from the stand-point of selfishness it was the natural thing for Great Britain to want. Viewed from the stand-point of self-preservation it was the most suicidal thing for a debtor nation to do. And yet it was done. Silver was demonetized, increasing all obligations by destroying one part of the money and making them payable alone in the other.

Great Britain at that time possessed India—poor,

wronged, plundered and vanquished India. At that time unprofitable and unproductive India. But there was a chance for Great Britain in India. Moses could "take of the water of the river, and pour it upon the dry land, and it became blood upon the dry land." And the Englishman found that he could take of the water of the river, and pour it upon the dry land, and it became wheat upon the dry land. There were plenty of Indian farmers whose agriculture was primitive and crude. The wooden mold-board plow and the white bulls were then as now the means of planting; the sickle and the flail finished the harvest. But India land watered by irrigation from the Indus, the Ganges and other of its great rivers, would produce wheat and cotton, and become a competitor with the United States in the markets of the world. Could England make it profitable to develope the vast plains of that historic country? The Indian farmer was willing to grow a bushel of wheat for so much silver. His coin was an Indian rupee. It was all the money he knew or cared to know. "A primrose on the river's brim, a yellow primrose was to him, and it was nothing more." A rupee to the Indian farmer, a silver rupee, was to him, and it was nothing more—and nothing less. It was wholly immaterial to him whether his rupee was made from silver that cost his British customer $1.30 an ounce or 60 cents an ounce. It was a silver rupee, and was a satisfactory measure of value to him. By just so much as the Englishman could cheapen silver, by that same process he could cheapen Indian wheat and cotton, and with them American wheat and cotton. The scheme worked, and for twenty years, more and more thoroughly every year, the India farmer has been made the competitor of the American farmer in growing wheat and cotton—made the competitor because the United States made it possible for him to be.

And so, since 1873, the American farmer has been compelled to raise his wheat and cotton and sell them on a falling market. The price of these two commodities have marched in a sort of a lock-step with degraded silver through all these twenty years. There are those who say they can see no existing relation between the price of silver on the one hand and wheat and cotton on the other. They cannot see it because they will not. But most certain it is that while silver, as measured by the gold standard, has decreased in value since 1873 from about $1.30 an ounce to its present price of about 60 cents, the price of wheat in the New York market as averaged by the year has fallen from almost precisely the same maximum to the same minimum, and cotton has gone down from 20 cents to 8 cents. Of course there have been some little divergencies along the line of march, but the tendency has ever been downwards, and precisely the same downward distance has been reached by all. It is not claimed for a moment that these two commodities alone have been affected by the adverse silver legislation. It has fixed the prices to a greater or less degree for all commodities. Silver debasement has done its work all along the entire line of the productive industries. Mr. Edward B. Howell, in a splendid article in the October number of the "Review of Reviews," shows the frightful depreciation of all our leading commodities. His figures are from the Statistical Abstract of the United States, issued by the Bureau of Statistics under direction of the Secretary of the Treasury. His excellent article, with elaborate charts showing the utter ruin wrought to the American Producer, should be placed in the hand of every student of economic questions. From this article we see, among the other startling facts, that the cereal crop of the United States, being 1539 million bushels in 1873, worth 916 million dollars, had increased 50 per cent as to quantity in 1878, but was worth less than the crop of 1873. Up to 1888, the last year in which the figures are given, the cereal crop had increased over 1873 to the extent of 109 per cent, while the value increased only 44 per cent.

Perhaps no better illustration exists showing the sympathy between silver and our grain products than was furnished in 1890. In January of that year silver was worth 97 cents per ounce, wheat 75 cents and cotton about 10. In July the Sherman bill was passed—a poor excuse, but better than none. Immediately silver, as a commodity, advanced to $1.21 per ounce, wheat to about $1.10 and cotton to about 12½ cents.

From the discovery of America to 1849 the world's product of silver had been more than double that of gold—68½ per cent of silver to 31½ per cent of gold. This on authority of the monetary conference of 1876. At that time no man in America ever heard of the existence of too much silver—that it could not circulate on a parity with gold.

In 1849 the gold mines of California were discovered, and in 1851 those of Australia. These mines began to pour forth their wonderful wealth of the precious metal. For the first time in the world's history the value of the gold product far exceeded the silver product. By 1873 the relations existing between silver and gold had materially changed. In that year the silver proportion had fallen to 55 per cent and the gold proportion had risen to 45 per cent. Then it was that American statesmen found that there was too large a proportion of silver to be able to circulate with gold on a parity. It would maintain itself very well at 68½ per cent, but was no good when it had fallen to 55 per cent of the money metal. And so silver was demonetized in the interest of Great Britain and our own gold bug cormorants, to the destruction of nine-tenths of the industries of our people.

Silver demonetized! When? At a time when the great mines of this country had just been discovered. At a time when the wealth of the world lay at our feet. At a time when we heard the wonderful stories of our fabulous silver mines. At a time when the output of our gold mines was decreasing millions of dollars per annum. At a time when the creditor began to demand gold and the debtor was getting ready to pay the silver he had promised to pay. At a time when the borrower had bared his bosom to pay the pound of flesh and the usurer demanded the blood with it.

As before stated, it was natural, viewed from a purely selfish standpoint for Great Britain to want silver demonetized. It was natural for the money power of this country, always subservient to Great Britain and forming the most hateful aristocracy on earth, to want silver demonetized. It is natural now, from the same standpoint, for the same classes to adhere to their former policy, and it is despicable, dishonorable and infamous for the people to submit to the wrong.

Look at the picture! Great Britain and her colonies produce more gold than any other nation on earth, and comparatively little silver. The United States produces more silver than any other nation, and considerable gold. Great Britain's gold product exceeds her silver product each year in value more than 3 to 1. The silver product of the United States exceeds in value the gold product each year by more than 2 to 1. Great Britain can well afford to destroy her one part of silver in order to double the value of her three parts of gold. The United States destroys herself when she destroys her two parts of silver to enhance the value of her one part of gold. If this country must do something in the way of demonetization, let it try to be as wise as England—destroy the lesser in order to build up the greater. If she must destroy either of the precious metals, in the name of American justice let her rather destroy the 33 million dollars of annual gold product and save her 75 million dollars of silver. This would be wisdom compared to the other act, and infinitely less ruinous to the interests of the nation.

An object lesson: before demonetization, British Gold and Silver appear thus:

After demonetization, British Gold, doubling in value, appears thus:

British gain ⅓, thus:

Before demonetization, United States Gold and Silver appear thus:

After demonetization, U. S. Gold, doubling in value, appears thus:

U. S. loss 3-7, thus:

Great Britain, with her colonies, is a great wheat producer, and yields but little corn. The United States produces more corn than any other nation, as well as wheat. What if England, in order to enhance the value of her wheat for the benefit of her farmers, should forbid the use of corn as an article of food for man or beast? That ought to raise the value of her wheat, as the other has raised the price of her gold. But should the United States follow suit? Should she destroy her billion and a half bushels of corn production in order to advance the price of her half billion bushels of wheat product? And I submit it would be as wise for the United States to *defoodetize* the largest product of her farms as it is for her to demonetize the largest product of her mines.

They say we are pleading for silver which benefits alone the mine owner. There is not an agricultural state in the Union but would receive more benefit from silver coinage than could possibly result to any mining state. The enhanced prices which one great producing state would get for its products would benefit it more than all the benefits that could flow to all the mines in the United States.

They tell us the United States must follow the lead of the European nations in these matters of financial legislation, because we cannot go alone. The United States is great enough, and its industries sufficiently diversified, to be able to set the pace for the whole world. Let this nation with a big N, say to all the nations of the earth: "This white metal is money—it is our money—we mined it—we made it—it is good enough for us. Take it or leave it. And in the meantime be assured that we can get along very comfortably, thank you." This is wisdom and patriotism and protection with a big P, that beats all the tariff schedules for that purpose that were ever dreamed of. It is the sort of protection that people want, and the protection they will have, if they would worthily say:

> We are the sons of sires who baffled
> Crowned and mitered tyranny;
> They defied the field and scaffold
> For their birth-right, so will we.

CHAPTER XI.

RECAPITULATION AND PROPOSED REMEDIES.

The writer realizes that he has gone far beyond his original intentions in writing this treatise. It was intended to write as briefly as possible of some of the existing evils. In order to make such a book readable it must be short, for people, hungering for bread, will not take much time to read. And yet when one sets out to write earnestly on these matters there is such a vast field of wrongs to be righted that he can scarcely stop. This must be the author's apology for the unintended length he has given this discussion.

The reader has seen the wonderful Concentration of Wealth into the favored sections of the Union as shown in Chapter I. He has seen the equally wonderful Concentration into the hands of the favored classes, as shown in Chapter II.

In Chapter III he has seen many curious things connected with the Railroads of the country. The increased efficiency of Labor, the great profits of Capital, the wild stock-watering schemes, the cost of building railroads now, the present capitalization, the extortion practiced on the Producers, and many other particulars. It was there seen that this business with $4,000,000,000 of Capital, as represented by their original cost when labor and materials were high, in the last year of the Census decade made net profits of $360,000,000. That is, one-fifteenth of the wealth of the country invested in Railroads, took to itself nearly one-fifth of the wealth-gain.

Chapter IV was a consideration of the Banking interests. There it was seen that even National Banks, the peculiarly fostered and favored institutions of the Nation, had been rendered unsafe in the productive sections of the country by the destruction of the productive industries; that their successful money-making powers had been such that their stock had risen all the way from par for the least valuable up to 40 dollars for 1, for the most valuable; that their net earnings per year are 18 per cent, and that with less than one-sixtieth of the entire wealth of the country they are annually taking to themselves one-tenth of the entire wealth-gain.

In Chapter V we have a general consideration of the Manufacturing interests of the country. The magnificent profits of the 10 principal cities and of the 20 principal industries; the great increase in the capital invested in the business; some comparisons of their profit with the profit of their employees; a light touching of the tariff question, and the final discovery from actual official figures, that about one-ninth of the wealth of the

Nation invested in these great fields of industry took to itself three-fifths of the wealth-gain for 1890.

Here the reader may find a profitable object lesson which should be forever fixed upon his mind until the wrongs complained of shall be righted. Remember the entire wealth of the Nation is estimated to be about $60,000,000,000 of actual value. The gain from 1880 to 1890 was $2,000,000,000 per year. Then the matter will stand thus:

The Railroads of the country, with 4 billions of the National wealth, should have gained in 1890 this proportion of the entire wealth-gain ▬

They did gain ▬▬▬

The Banks, with 1 billion of the National wealth, should have gained in 1890 this proportion of the entire wealth-gain ▪

They did gain ▬▬

The Manufacturers, with 6½ billions of the National wealth, should have gained in 1890 this proportion of the wealth-gain ▬▬

They did gain ▬▬▬▬▬▬

All other people outside of the three favored classes, with about 48 billions of the entire National wealth, should have gained this proportion of the wealth-gain

▬▬▬▬▬▬▬▬▬▬▬▬

They did gain ▬▬

That is to say, all the people outside of the three favored classes, with about 48 billions of wealth were able to accumulate no more of the wealth-gain than the National Banks accumulated with 1 billion. The advantage in favor of the Banks was about 48 to 1. That ought to be more than enough to satisfy any greed.

Or, all the people outside of the three favored classes, with about 48 billions of wealth, were able to accumulate but little more than half as much as the Railroads accumulated with 4 billions.

Or, all the people outside of the three favored classes, with about 48 billions of wealth, were able to accumulate about one-sixth as much as the Manufacturers accumulated with 6½ billions. Does the reader not think it about time to call a halt?

After seeing these things, and seeing them from the official figures, and after contrasting the excessive profits of Railroad, Banking and Manufacturing interests with the losses of Labor, Farming and Trade as seen in Chapters VI, VII and VIII, the reader ought to be able to find the cause and be willing to apply some remedy.

What shall that remedy be? The writer is not very particular on that question. Looking back over the past the intelligent student of economic questions can discover the causes that have produced all the evil results. His remedy should be generally to undo everything in financial legislation that has been done in the last twenty years. A new financial policy must be the heroic treatment for a desperate disease. It is all the platform the people need. Upon this they should agree. Everything, for the past twenty years has been done for the benefit of the favored Classes as against the oppressed Masses. The wrongs done by vicious legislation can only be cured by undoing them. The rights undone can only be remedied by doing them. As the Masses have been oppressed for twenty years it will only be restoring them to their own to let them find favorable legislation for twenty years to come. The same power that wrongfully legislated property away from the people can and should legislate it back again. This is not injustice. It is the acme of fair-dealing and impartial justice. It will not do to let the despoiler, shielding himself forever under the law which he made, protect himself in wrong-doing.

To carry out this proposed platform and do everything of financial legislation in an opposite manner in which it has been done we find the following proposed remedies:

Instead of depreciating the value of the results of all productive industry by contracting the currency, they should be restored to their former values by expansion of the circulating medium.

Instead of wealth belonging to him who has the power to take it, we should recognize the rights of him who creates it. "In the sweat of thy face shalt thou eat bread" must not be longer construed as authority for one to eat the bread that many have earned.

Railroads are public highways, not private. The

state has no power to confer on Railroad corporations the right to take private property—that is, your home for their roadway—unless it is taken for *public* purposes. The policy of the Railroads owning and operating the Government should be changed into that of the Government owning and operating the Railroads, as its other public highways, for the benefit of all the people.

Instead of the National Banks absolutely controlling the financial affairs of the Nation by expanding or contracting the currency at will, a National currency should be issued by the general government, without the intervention of National Banks.

Instead of collecting the revenue of the Government wholly from the consumer without reference to his ability to pay, as has been done under the "Protection" system, a graduated income tax should be imposed in order that the rich may bear a more equitable portion of the burdens of taxation.

Instead of bestowing the public lands of the country on the great corporations as has been done in the past, all such lands that have not passed into the hands of *bonafide* settlers should be reclaimed and held for settlement by the homeless poor of the country.

The rights of Labor must be more thoroughly recognized than ever before. Improved machinery is constantly lessening the time necessarily consumed in manufacture. Labor-saving machinery always lessening human toil, Labor should receive its proportionate share of the benefits in reduced hours, thereby the better fitting itself for more exalted citzenship. Men say this class of legislation cannot be made effective. Why not? The world furnishes no precedent for such legislation, we are told. History furnishes no precedent for such a world as we have now. Since the opening era of steam, the changes wrought are greater than all others since the birth of Christ. It requires new legislation to meet new wants in a new world. Americans boast of the high wages of American Labor. If its wages are higher it is because its accomplishment is greater. This is shown in the quotation from Governor Larrabee on a preceding page. Hon. James G. Blaine, Secretary of State in his letter to Congress on the Commercial Relations of the United States, in 1881, said;

> "Undoubtedly the inequalities in the wages of English and American operatives are more than equalized by the greater efficiency of the latter and their longer hours of labor. If this should prove to be a fact in practice, as it seems to be proven from official statistics, it would be a very important element in the establishment of our ability to compete with England for our share of the cotton-goods trade of the world."

And it seems to be a fact in practice. Dr. E. R. L. Gould, one of the Professors of Johns Hopkins University, is one of the most accomplished statisticians in the United States. Dr. Gould spent some years in charge of the European side of the Labor Question, in the employ of the United States Department of Labor. In an excellent magazine article recently published, he says:

"Speaking broadly and generally, one may say that labor which is paid by the day always receives a much higher compensation in the United States than in any foreign country. When, however, piecework prevails, that is, when quantity and not time is made the unit of payment, we frequently find that the rates established do not vary considerably. Take, for example, the price paid weavers for weaving print cloth. In Massachusetts it is about 40 cents per 100 yards; in England the price is practically the same; in France 44 cents for a similar unit of measure; and in Germany 43 cents. But the daily earnings of weavers, weaving this particular class of fabric varies in somewhat the following proportions: in Massachusetts $1.15; in England $1.02; in France 60 cents; in Germany 55 cents. The explanation of the fact lies in this, that the American weaver runs six looms; the British four at a higher rate of speed; the French as a rule, two; and the German the same number. Here is a case, and there are not lacking many others, which personal investigation may easily disclose, showing that enhanced earnings are due to greater effort on the part of the laborer, *who under these circumstances becomes a cheaper workman to his employer.*"

The Railroads and the Manufacturers of the country employ about 6 million wage-earners. Suppose the hours of labor were reduced sufficiently to give employment to 2 millions more who belong to the great army of unemployed. This could be done without reducing wages, and still the Railroads and Manufacturers *would get more than their share of the profits of the country.*

Instead of taxing out the products of pauper labor of Europe by the alleged Protection of American Labor in high tariff robbery, bar out undesirable labor by such legislation as will be in fact a protection.

Instead of fostering corporations, trusts and combines, repeal or radically amend all laws for the creation of corporations, and let such vast enterprises as are too large for the individual be operated by the state or municipality. Make it a felony for any man or set of men to enter into a conspiracy with other men in forming any trust or combination looking to the control of any part of the commerce of the country. Such enactment honestly passed and faithfully enforced would protect the Producer from the arbitrary prices fixed by monopolists. With such laws Iowa meat packers would not testify as they did before a Senatorial Investigating Committee four years ago that Kansas City packers paid an agreed price per head for all live stock that would naturally go to the Iowa houses, provided the Iowa packers would close their plants. With such restrictive laws the Kansas City packers would no longer find it necessary to charge up to one year's operating expenses more than 3 million dollars as "Sundries not elsewhere reported."

Instead of dishonoring and debasing one of the largest products of the industries of the country—the one mineral of greater value than all the other minerals combined—let the people of all the producing sections of the country demand the full remonetization of silver on the basis of 16 to 1, and accept no compromise with the Money Power. Let the people demand free coinage of silver, not because it is the best means of relief, but because it is most speedy. Then, perhaps, after the people shall have thought along these lines (and they are thinking as they never have thought before) they will see how much more sensible it would be for the Government to make a piece of paper a dollar rather than a piece of metal. Instead of wasting a day to find a bit of silver from which to make a dollar, let the workman apply his energy to the useful employment of building roads and bridges, and receive the best dollar for it that ever was made—a paper one, based on the faith of the greatest nation on earth. But until that time let the waste of labor go on in finding silver—the next best thing to a paper dollar. But it will be a "fiat" dollar all the same. So will a gold dollar, or any other dollar made of any other metal or thing. So long as the "fiat" of the Government is necessary to make it a dollar so long it will continue to be "fiat," just as thoroughly as the little piece of paper.

But the purpose of this work is to present facts, not the opinions of the writer. A brave people knowing their rights will ever dare to maintain them. Knowing their wrongs they will find a way to right them. What the forged arm was for the defense of the Englishman the intelligent ballot should be to the American. Seventy years ago the great Shelly told his countrymen of their wrongs and the way to right them. They were brave words to fling in the face of royalty:

> The seed ye sow another reaps:
> The wealth ye find another keeps;
> The robes ye weave another wears;
> The arms ye forge another bears.
>
> Sow seed,—but let no tyrant reap;
> Find wealth,—let no imposter heap;
> Weave robes,—let not the idle wear;
> Forge arms,—in your defense to bear.

GOV. GREENHALGE AND THE BOSTON CRY FOR WORK.

CONCLUSION.

A SCENE FROM A NEW PLAY.

Place, *State House Steps, Boston.* Time, *February 20, A. D. 1894.*
Enter a thousand hungry citizens, without staves, clubs or other weapons.

Citizen Swift. We have made propositions for work on state farms and factories. Something must be done. The case is urgent. We cannot go on starving. We have come for assistance to the place where the laws are made.

Gov. Greenhalge. To the Executive you come,
And he's a servant too. The Governor
Declares his hand unable is to help
The poor. The major part of all our men
Have food, and hunger not. Shall these be made
to bear the burden of your lives, and give
You work to win your bread, while they receive
No gain? It must not be. I'd fain do all
That man may do, but strictly in the law.
'Tis better far that men should starve and save
The law than that our laws should bend to man.
'T would be recorded for a precedent,
And many an error by the same example
Would rush into the state. It cannot be.

Citizen Casson. In times like these precedents should be thrown to the winds. While the officials are stickling over precedents the unemployed are losing their respect for the laws. If this official and governmental neglect continues, I don't like to look forward to what may happen.

Gov. G. Make me no threats. From you and such as you
No terrors come. In me and such as me
No terrors lodge. I am too great for fear.
You ask for work which this great state can't give.
A government of laws, not men, this is,
And laws, not men, our sacred care must be.
No public work—no help—the state can give
Unless it need the work—not you the wage;
Unless some benefit it gains—not you;
Unless it hath the weal—not you the woe;*
What's your further seeking. 'Tis told you dared
To say that from these halls myself and my
Associates shall be driven.

Citizen Swift. I said it should be done with the ballot.

Gov. G. I like not words like these. Obnoxious are
Their sounds, and not for toleration here.
I warn you now, if trouble comes, yourself
Responsible, shall drink the dregs of woe.

Exeunt from the State House the hungry citizens who hold a further meeting on the Commons and thence supperless to bed.

Scene 2. Place, *Banquet Hall.* Time, *The Night of Feb. 20, 1894.*

The curtain rises slowly, discovering the Life Insurance Presidents at their annual banquet, a blaze of brilliant light falling on rich furnishings and sumptous viands. The band plays, "Hail to the Chief." Enter Governor Greenhalge.

Gov. G. Myself immortal I have made.
From stormy scenes I come. 'Tis here I come
To ask support from order-loving men.
Such rights we freely give to ev'ry child
Of man that lives, that he an equal chance
May have with all. And when this banquet board

---

* The author condemns the law more strongly than he condemns the Governor. The state can take from the citizen his liberty, his labor—even his life. It should have power to grant the means of living to those whose life it hath the power to take.

CONCLUSION. 143

I view, it boiling sets my blood to think
That any hungry man may feel or say
Our Massachusetts is unjust to men.
   The Presidents all shout.
   Gov. G. And when I see dissentious crowds like those
I met to-day, I ask myself how long
Before our state shall give its answer forth
That men must uncomplaining stand or fall,
And not repine because they think our laws
Unequal or unfriendly are to them.
   The Presidents all shout again.
   Gov. G. We simply want our loyal men and those
Who Lives insure; and business men, to stand
By Massachusetts now. And you are they
On whom we lean, and leaning thus on you,
We'll pass through all our troublous times as through
The mists the sunbeams pass

The Presidents all cheer three times three. The banquet finished, they go forth to mingle again with the busy world in their honest vocations of suborning perjury and hiring witnesses in order to defeat such claims for death-losses as are large enough to warrant the effort. Boston continues to prosper, but—her hungry are still unfed.

It is not claimed that the above is a verbatim report of Governor Greenhalge's two Boston speeches. It is insisted, however, that the spirit of his remarks, both at the state house and at the banquet, on that eventful day, has been faithfully portrayed. If the reader thinks the author has drawn too much on his imagination for the above scenes, let him send for a copy of the Boston Herald, of February 21, 1894.

www.ingramcontent.com/pod-product-compliance
Lightning Source LLC
Chambersburg PA
CBHW030355170426
43202CB00010B/1380